$14⁹⁵ U.S.
$19⁹⁵ CANADA

A COLLECTOR'S GUIDE TO
NESTING DOLLS
HISTORIES, IDENTIFICATION, VALUES

by
Michele Lyons Lefkovitz

To my dear husband, Paul,
who started my nesting doll
collection and encouraged me
to write this book.

To my children, Alison and Steven,
who share my love for the fine
nested dolls.

To my parents, Bette & Daniel J. Lyons Jr.,
for their love and support.

BOOKS AMERICANA
INC

ISBN 0-89689-069-4

TABLE OF CONTENTS

Acknowledgements

This book could not have been written without the assistance, support and generosity of many people. I will try to thank each and every one of them here. My wonderful husband, Paul, was so instrumental in every aspect of this book. He first encouraged me to write it several years ago, after many years of collecting. Paul was also very much involved in the preparation of the manuscript. He functioned as chief editor, loving supporter, computer consultant and assistant typist at times. He has my eternal love and thanks. I also want to offer thanks to my dear friend, Terri Shackelford, for her editorial assistance, the photographs she took, and her abundant support. I extend thanks to my friend, Barbara Boal, who kept my spirits up when I felt the task was just too overwhelming.

Wanda Martz of The Copper Coin in Carlisle, Ohio deserves special acknowledgement as the one who first introduced me to the world of nesting dolls in the early 1970's. I found her buoyant enthusiasm for folk figurines to be contagious and my life has never been quite the same since.

Natalie Polzin of The Little House Boutique in Indianapolis, Indiana has kindly allowed me to photograph sets of nesting dolls in her shop. Natalie has always been kind, cooperative and has kept me informed of current developments in the field. Kathryn Wright of The Bittersweet Boutique in Nashville, Indiana also graciously allowed me to photograph dolls in her shop. Kathryn introduced me to Marion Zeiger, President of Shelmar Imports Ltd., the leading importer of Soviet Matreshkas. Vitaly Shukin of Maison Russe, a Russian curio and gift shop in Lisle, Illinois allowed me to photograph sets from his shop and provided other photographs and valuable information concerning different doll types. To Wanda, Natalie, Kathryn, and Vitaly, I extend my sincerest appreciation.

I am particularly grateful to Marion Zeiger of Shelmar Imports Ltd. Marion contacted me several years ago to inquire about this book while it was in its infancy. Without her helpful encouragement, this book probably never would have been completed.

I want to thank Judy Ryan and Ron Gibson of The Children's Museum of Indianapolis. They graciously allowed me to view and photograph dolls from the spectacular Caplan Collection, which consists of 50,000 pieces of folk art, crafts and toys from around the world.

I greatly appreciate the enjoyable time spent with Zoya and Gennady Plotkin. These unselfish friends, native Russians, but now American citizens, provided valuable information concerning the stories and histories of the folkcraft.

I have met many enthusiastic collectors while writing this book. Many of them generously allowed me to photograph sets from their collections. I wish to thank the following collectors: Molly M. Cava, Kimberly R. Knight, my children, Alison L. and Steven C. Lefkovitz, Jackie, Kelly and Molly Parker, Linda S. Prell, Teresa L. Shackelford and Maria Spratford of Indianapolis. I extend thanks to my Mother, Bette M. Lyons of Cincinnati, Ohio, Olga and Vitaly Shukin of Lisle, Illinois and Eleanor B. Wilson of Hilton Head, South Carolina. Helen Daum of Plainfield, Indiana allowed me to photograph her cousin's collection (the late Lois M. Zimmerman). Frances S. and Laura Killen also allowed me to photograph their collections, a part of which also had belonged to Miss Zimmerman. Many thanks to these three ladies.

I want to thank Pam Barry, Linda and Steve Cannon and Pam Miksch with help they provided concerning the manuscript. Special thanks to my publisher, Dan Alexander of Books Americana for his helpful assistance, his cheerfulness and support.

Finally, I want to express my deepest thanks to my family for their unending patience, love, support and understanding as I spent countless hours photographing dolls, writing and typing at the computer. To Paul, Alison and Steven, I extend my love and heartfelt thanks.

Introduction

In our modern world of high technology, mechanization, computers, industrialization, speed and mass production, it is a joy to seek and find simple pleasures. People yearn for less complicated ways to relate to one another. Collecting hand crafted items has met this need for many people.

A growing group of collectors find the nesting doll sets of yesteryear refreshing. The dolls are simple, yet lovely, humble yet rich in personality. These unique, hand-made folk dolls, created by common artisans, are produced in at least thirteen different countries. In the last fifteen years or so, Americans, in particular, have discovered the secret hidden treasures of nested dolls.

Nesting doll sets were rarities in the United States prior to the 1970's. Americans were unfamiliar with folk nesting dolls and no published references were available about the subject. Today, in contrast, the dolls are much more readily available. Their increased availability parallels the rapidly mushrooming interest among American collectors in this fascinating field.

This truly is an exciting new arena, wide open to collectors. An expansive array of types, styles, and sizes are imported into the United States every year from a number of countries. New types are eagerly awaited each season by enthusiastic collectors. The American public today is quite familiar with the concept of nesting dolls. The sets are becoming more ubiquitous, appearing in ads, cartoons, magazine covers and film clips.

The concept of nesting dolls has an extensive history going back at least 900 years. Nested folk boxes were first invented in China about 1000 A.D. In the early 1800's, the Chinese created the first wooden nesting dolls as we know them today. The early Chinese sets were thinly turned and grotesquely lacquered. The smallest doll in the set was a grain of rice. The development of nesting dolls was furthered considerably in Russia as the concept spread West. In the latter part of the 19th century, Russian artist, Sergei Malyutin sketched the first Russian nested doll. Master carver, V. Zveydochin turned the dolls on a wood lathe, while Malyutin painted the first set himself. These pioneering Zveydochin Matreshka dolls are on permanent display at the Museum of Toys in Zagorsk. The Matreshka's popularity extended beyond the borders of that country after being displayed in the Paris World's Exhibition in 1900. A few years later, in the early 1900's, Vevgenny Bezrukov created a set of 70 dolls, handcarved from a lime tree. This set has been exhibited at three World's Fairs. In the 1920's, exports of nesting dolls from Russia increased dramatically with the opening of a major production center in Zagorsk. About this same time, nesting dolls were being made by German toymakers in and around Munich. The craft did not flourish there, but continued to prosper in Russia and Poland. It wasn't until the late 1950's and early 1960's that the Soviet dolls were becoming well known outside their own country. In more recent years, other countries have "flattered" the Russians by imitating the nesting dolls, while introducing distinctive characteristics reflective of their own cultures.

Nesting dolls are most often made of lathe turned hardwoods. In the past, some sets were hand-carved. A few plastic sets can even be found. However, hand painted wooden sets most effectively reveal the artisan's skill and are the most desirable. Nesting dolls characteristically split in half to reveal another, smaller doll, and yet another in diminishing sizes. However, this book will describe numerous interesting and delightful variations on that basic theme.

Nesting dolls are primarily sought out by adult collectors. The Russian types are particularly popular with adults since they are very artistic, detailed, delicate and varied. Yet children also love the Russian dolls. They enjoy nesting and unnesting the sets, arranging and rearranging them for hours. Other countries, however, produce less expensive, sturdier sets that better serve that purpose.

The emergence of nesting dolls as a popular collector's item, interestingly, has not been accompanied by readily available published reference materials. This book was therefore written to meet the growing need for information about this fascinating subject. It is intended as a comprehensive reference and identification guide. Over two hundred distinct types of nesting dolls are described and pictured on the pages to follow. However, it is recognized that this guide does not include every nested doll and toy ever made.

For those of you who are avid collectors, you already understand the delight that went into writing this volume. The author hopes new collectors will soon catch the fever and experience all of the excitement this hobby has to offer!

Value Guide

Many aspects need to be considered when placing a value on nesting doll sets. As a general rule, the more dolls in a set, the greater the value. The size of the largest doll is an important factor in determining the overall value of a set as well. In larger Russian sets, the general rule of thumb is that the addition of a larger doll to a set will increase the value of the set by up to 50%. For example, a Semenov set of 10 will cost $100 while a set of 11 will be $150. Wooden dolls are generally more desirable and valuable than plastic ones. Older sets are worth more, because they are more difficult to find. Often, the more detail the set has, the greater the value. Detail includes painted designs, lathe work, woodburning, carving and inlays of wheat, mother-of-pearl and wood. Some sets are worth more because they were made in limited quantities. Other sets are valuable because they are unavailable in the United States.

On the other hand, there are factors that reduce the value of a set. If a wooden doll is cracked, the set is worth less. The painting on each doll should be carefully rendered. Chipped or peeling paint makes a set worth less. On the other hand, faded paint does not seem to greatly devalue the dolls. Most paint does fade over a period of time. Incomplete sets with missing dolls are less valuable. When a set is unnested, the dolls decrease in a standard progression. If there is a large size decrepency, suspect a missing doll. The smallest doll in a nesting set is usually solid and does not open. If the smallest doll of a set does open, there is a smaller doll missing. The one exception to this guideline can be found in a group of three-piece sets manufactured by Kubla Crafts in the early 1980's. Improper fit of the doll halves can devalue the set. Dolls should all fit well together so that no internal wood shows at the seam. Likewise, when you pick up a doll, both pieces should be a unit. If the bottom falls off, the fit is poor. The dolls should also fit inside one another.

When purchasing old sets of nesting dolls, different rules apply. Incomplete sets are the norm. Paint on old sets will usually be faded and sometimes chipped. Cracks in old sets are not the problem they are in new sets. There may be any one of three different identification markings on old Soviet sets which can help determine the date of origin. Dolls marked ''Made in Russia'' were made before 1917. The marking ''Made in the Soviet Union'' is the second category. ''Made in the U.S.S.R.'' appeared after 1924. This marking is still used even today. The earliest made sets are worth the most, if they are in good condition.

Most of the prices in this guide reflect current, retail prices. If a nesting dolls set is found in perfect shape, it is worth the higher amount in the range. Often a retailer will negotiate a lower price if a doll in the set has some damage.

U.S.S.R.

The U.S.S.R. is a country vast in size and varied in culture. It is truly a land of contrasts. From sub-zero weather in Siberia to tropical temperatures in the southern regions, we find great extremes. It is a land so vast, the sun never sets.

Within this large country, we find varied ethnic, cultural and racial groups. No other country in the world has Russia's great variety of people. The largest group, including the Great Russians, Belorussians and Ukrainians are Slavs. The Slavs form three quarters of the population. The Turkic people, the second largest group, are the descendants of the Tartars who invaded Russia in the thirteenth century. The Soviet peoples also include Armenians, Georgians, Finns, Latvians, Kurds, Tadzhiks and Eskimos. The Soviet people have survived centuries of invasions, wars and revolutions. The universal language of man, the arts and crafts of the country, have also survived.

The folk arts of Russia have diverse forms, each region reflecting its own ethnic flavor. Probably the best known and most popular Soviet folk art today is the brightly painted, lathe turned, Matreshka* nesting doll. Every region of the Russian Federation has an ambition to produce its own unique Matreshka. The tremendous variations in Soviet Matreshkas are seen in the shapes, paint styles and sizes of the different sets.

In the late 1800's, a Russian artist, Sergei Malyutin sketched the first ''Russian'' Matreshka. Perhaps Malyutin was familiar with the legendary, great woman goddess, Jumala. She was once worshipped in Ancient Ugria, a forrested country in the foothills of the Ural Mountains. Legends say she was a statue of pure gold with a hollow interior. Jumala contained three figures, one inside the other. No one has ever found the hidden goddess, but the legend persists. Other sources suggest the Matreshka represents the archetypical woman goddess who protects all hearths. This woman goddess is not one and the same as Jumala of Ancient Ugria. Still another source says, Malyutin was inspired by a set of Japanese Darumas nested inside each other and hand carved. The set had been brought to the Moscow toy workshop of Savva Morozov in the late nineteenth century. Morozov was an industrialist and patron of the arts. It is said that Malyutin liked the figures and designed his set based on the Japanese sage, Daruma. Perhaps all the sources were correct and Malyutin was inspired by several ideas. Whatever the origin, the end result was the first Matreshka.

Malyutin had the skilled turner and mastercarver, V. Zveydochin turn the dolls on a wood lathe from his sketches. Malyutin, himself hand painted the set of eight dolls. This first Matreshka set still survives today on permanent display at the Museum of Toys in Zagorsk. Six of the figures were girls, one a boy, and the smallest was a swaddled baby. All the girls wore babushkas or kerchiefs on their heads. The largest doll carried a black rooster under her arm. One girl held a sickle, one carried a bowl and a small girl sucked her thumb. Unlike the brightly painted Matreshkas of today, this first set was painted in subdued earth tones.

In the early 1900's, the craftsmen of Semenov in the Gorky district imitated Malyutin's set and created their own style. These Semenov sets have become the classical, traditional dolls one thinks of when Matreshkas come to mind. Other regions eventually developed their own versions of the nested doll, with variations reflective of their people and cultures.

The Matreshka ranks first among Russian wooden souvenirs. Russian toys are famous, and Moscow's biggest toy shop, Detsky Mir (Children's World) has shelves of these unique, diminutive, Matreshka dolls. Oddly enough, most Matreshkas are sold as tourist souvenirs or are exported for sale abroad. The Russian people do give the Matreshkas as gifts to newborn infants and children. However, Russian adults do not collect Matreshka dolls in the same way that American adult collectors do.

In the United States, the Soviet Matreshkas have become quite popular. In the last fifteen years, Matreshkas from many different regions have been imported into the United States. There is increasing interest among collectors who are very serious about acquiring the Soviet dolls from all different districts. Two articles have appeared in the *Doll Reader* magazine providing information about the Matreshka dolls. The articles, ''Matreoschka'' by Ann Bahar, Dec. 1984/Jan. 1985, and ''The Russian Nested Doll'' by Linda Poirer Holderbaum, Aug./Sept. 1985 have whetted the appetites of American collectors for more information about these favorite dolls.

In her article, Ann Bahar writes about old Russian Matreshka sets and provides an unusual glimpse into the earliest days of Matreshka production. She gives us fifteen examples of early sets that clearly reflect this nineteenth century art form. The author has never seen examples of these sets. Likewise, their specific origins are not known. Probably, most of these sets hale from Zagorsk, Semenov or Polkhov Maidan, because these were the earlist centers of Matreshka manufacture. What a wonderful find for a collector to locate an early set! Ann Bahar describes the sets for us in a way that makes them come alive. There were Matreshka sets of girls wearing short sheepskin coats, shawls and felt boots. Sets of Shepherdesses with reed pipes nested snugly. Early sets of old men with beards, and old believers and nuns with rosaries in their hands were created by craftsmen of pre-communist Russia. Who could resist a lovely bride and groom with candles and relatives nested inside? Sets of Noblemen (Boyars) and their wives dressed in fur coats and high fur hats were made while there still was a Russian nobility. More common Clerks with inkpots were nested. Falconers and warriors were also nested. Unique sets that commemorated special events were made

---

*Russian spelling, Matryoshka; Polish spelling, Matroszka.   3

in the early part of this century. Two examples are the Jubilee characters from the Gogol Centenary, and the Russian General, Mikhail Kutuzov and Napoleon with staff officers (1912). The last four sets described by Ann Bahar are interpretations of Russian fairy trales. There is a turnip man, his wife and granddaughter, dog, cat and mouse all nested together. The golden fish, and the wonderbird are two fairy tale sets. Last, but not least is Czarevitch Ivan. Collectors today should be aware of the Matreshka's past history to fully understand the current and future Matreshka sets.

The Matreshka dolls of today and in times past, have been manufactured in much the same way. The dolls are lathe turned of seasoned Linden wood, a form of pine. Lime tree wood is turned less often than the more common Linden wood. Both wood types are rather soft and easily turned on a lathe. The larger the piece of wood, the bigger the set is. The most common misconception is that the dolls in one set must all come from the same block of wood. This is untrue, yet the dolls give that impression as they snuggly nest inside each other. The lathe turners hollow out many dolls of the same uniform size in an assembly fashion. They are later combined into sets where each doll diminishes as the set grows. One set may contain the work of several artists. The most common number of dolls in a set are 3, 7 and 12. There are sets of 1, 2, 3, 4, 5, 6, 7, 8, 9, 10, 11, 12, 14, 16, 18, 24, 48 and even 70 dolls. These sets come in many varied shapes as well.

Two definitions have been given for the term "Matreshka." The nesting dolls are a traditional gift for newborn infants in this slavic culture, implying fertility, eternal life and timelessness. Woman is the vessel of new life. She contains succeeding generations within herself. The name Matreshka has been said to mean "Grandmother." Several reasons are given for this. First, Russian grandmothers often wear kerchiefs or babushkas, which many Matreshka dolls wear. Second, the largest doll in a set represents the oldest woman in a family. Often she is the grandmother. Finally, grandparents traditionally handcarved the dolls for their grandchildren. Usually the grandfather carved or turned the dolls and the grandmother painted the sets. Today the dolls are all lathe made. In actuality, "Babushka" is the Russian name for grandmother.

A second definition has been given for the term "Matreshka." The name, Mastryona, an old Russian name, is a common one for women in country villages. She is the village mother of all the children. The dolls were named for her in the endearing form – dear Matresha or darling Matresha. The closest English equivalent is "Dear Martha."

Each region will be described in terms of its location in the Soviet Union and the Matreshka dolls it produces. Detailed descriptions of the doll types are given.

SEMENOV

The Semenov Matreshka dolls are the most traditional and classical nesting doll sets. After Malyutin's prototype, the Semenov dolls were first made in the early 1900's. They have undergone several stylistic changes through the years. Today the sets are bright and vibrant. The Semenov dolls are the most commonly found Matreshka sets.

The Semenov village is located in the Gorky region (Voznesensk District) of Russia, northeast of Moscow and due north of Gorky. The Semenov dolls produced there are very bright and broad. The head takes up nearly half of the doll. The face is very large with refined features. The Semenov Matreshka dolls are rendered in oil paint and black india ink. The natural color of the wood is used for skin tones. The eyes are very distinctive; they are always black with a line above and beneath the pupil. A wood toned, natural dot in the pupil and a natural wood area around the pupil designates the iris. Arched thin brows lie above the eye. On very large dolls, eyelashes are sometimes added. Two small black dots depict the nose. A sweet pink mouth and large, dark, pink dots as healthy cheeks are rendered. Semenov dolls always have black hair parted in the middle. The maidens wear a kerchief or babushka on their heads. Most often the babushkas are yellow, but sometimes black "fingerprint" swirls are imprinted over the yellow.

The Semenov maidens always carry a gay bouquet of garden flowers, mostly poppies and tulips in shades of red, purple and pinks. On occasion, bright red roses make up the bouquet. The bouquets of some large sets have luscious red strawberries mixed in with the flowers. The Semenov dresses are primarily red. Less often a deep purple is chosen. The features of the dolls including hands and aprons are drawn in black, thin lines.

The Semenov maidens are the most common dolls. They can be found in sets of one through fourteen, 16, 18, 24, 25, 48, 50 and 70! In addition to the basic nesting doll theme, there are three variations of this Semenov maiden. The first variation is a bowling set. It consists of a large Semenov maiden with two colorful, wooden bowling balls and nine figures inside. The eight pins are thin, solid Semenov maidens, while the head pin is a boy dressed in a yellow shirt and red cap with purple trousers. The second variation is a counting set. It consists of a smaller Semenov maiden with ten, small, solid maidens inside. The solid maidens are all the same size and do not nest inside each other. The third variation is a set of 52 solid dolls. Fifty of the dolls are miniature, similar to the counting set. The other two dolls are somewhat larger, one dressed in red and the other in purple. They do not nest inside one another. This set is rarely, if ever, found outside the Soviet Union. It was carried into the U.S.A. by immigrants.

A chef counting set is also produced by the Semenov craftsmen. This set is similar to the maiden counting set in that it consists of a large male chef with ten small, solid chefs inside. Again, the solid chefs are all the same size and do not nest inside each other. The large male chef does not display typical Semenov features. He has blue round eyes and a red round mouth. A large black mustache lies above the mouth. One large, red, stylized flower decorates the front of his natural wood body. He wears a white chef's hat and blue clothing. He is quite unusual and modern in appearance.

The Semenov craftsmen have created two other counting sets. Like the maiden and chef sets, they consist of a large hollow figure with ten solid small figures inside. The cat and chicken (sometimes called the toy) counting sets were both new in the United States in 1986. These new animal counting sets are very unusual as Semenov themes.

The cat and chicken are quite unique as humanized animals. The cat is dressed as a typical Russian man. He has a natural wood tone head with no ears. Large green eyes, a red nose and large black whiskers define his face. The cat wears a red cap with a black bill. The cap is accented with black, swirl fingerprints. His jacket is bright red, while his trousers are coal black. The natural, wood tone shirt is decorated with a single, large red flower and greenery. Inside are ten male kittens dressed in red caps, yellow shirts, red bowties and black trousers. Like the chef, the cat is very modern in appearance.

The chicken, in contrast to the cat, is a very feminine, mother hen. She has large, round, orange eyes and a red comb. Her natural wood tone breast, face and beak complement her bright yellow head and wings. Black, swirl fingerprints cover the head and wings. Mother hen wears a bright red cloak. A lovely red flower complete with greenery accents her breast. Ten, small simple yellow chicks nest inside. These counting sets are modern variations of the traditional Semenov sets. Probably new versions will appear in the future.

Two, very large 14″ elongated Semenov bottle holders are manufactured to contain wine or vodka bottles. One is a traditional Semenov maiden. She is unique becuase her base is removable. The maiden does not split in the middle as her other Matreshka sisters do. A large bottle is set inside the base and the body of the doll fits over the base. Her companion is a Russian young man. He is similar to the older Polkhov Maidan boy boxes. The Semenov man is dressed in a red cap, black trousers and a natural wood shirt. The shirt is decorated at the neckline and hem with small red flowers and greenery. He carries a bouquet of bright red flowers. Unlike the maiden, the man splits in half as traditional Matreshkas do. In 1987, two new 14″ bottle holders were introduced. The maiden is more elaborate than the original and the man now opens at the bottom as well. These four bottle holders are made with the same care and skill as the traditional Matreshka maidens.

A smaller set of 8″ bottle holders are made in Semenov. The young man greatly resembles the larger male with two exceptions. His red cap is of a different shape. The cap is decorated with flowers and has a black bill. This young man is very unusual for a Semenov, because he has orange hair. It appears that the greatest deviations occur with the male figures. The maiden bottle holder in this set is quite lovely. On top of her head rests a yellow crown decorated with flowers and black swirl fingerprints. Her babushka is trimmed with black fringe. She also wears a red vest. The fringe, vest and crown are very unusual for a Semenov maiden. This set if very beautiful and functional as well.

The traditional Semenov dolls often did not include men. There are two sets of Semenov Male Matreshka sets that are available today. The first set is based on a poem by the Russian poet, Alexander Pushkin. The dolls are commonly known as the Vikings or Tartar warriors. In actuality, they are neither. The Russian warriors represent the thirty-three warriors Pushkin described in his poem. The Chief was called "Black Sea." These thirty-three warriors lived in the depths of the ocean. Anytime they were needed to defend the Russian countryside, they were called up. Black Sea was the largest warrior and the other warriors diminished in size as the numbers got larger. The Matreshka set is designed exactly as Pushkin described the men.

The Russian warrior Matreshka comes in two sizes, four or five figures. They have the traditional Semenov face with two exceptions, bushy eyebrows and mustaches. They also wear wood tone long beards. The men wear red, onion shaped helmets. The chief, Black Sea, carries a red shield and a yellow club in his purple "bead" hand. Their uniforms consist of yellow, "fingerprinted" tunics, yellow belts and purple trousers. The warriors appear quite fierce.

The second male Matreshka set is a combination of males and females. It is, in fact, a family. This set of four, called the Good Family Man, includes a father, mother, son and daughter. The father wears a yellow coat decorated with small red flowers on the lapels. He has a red cap on his head with "fingerprinted" designs that depict fur. His facial features are true Semenov with the exception of his short beard. The mother is a traditional maiden. The son is a miniature verison of the large male bottle holder. Finally, the daughter resembles the maidens, but wears a cap and coat instead of a babushka and dress. This Good Family Man is the only modern, Russian family set the author is aware of.

Two small, Semenov egg sets are available, usually in the spring. The first set includes three egg maidens. They are all natural wood with swirl "fingerprints" of black or red covering their babushkas and dresses. The eyes and hair are rendered in a slightly varied way. The egg maidens are not nearly as detailed as the regular maiden sets. The second egg set consists of a natural wood colored egg with red flowers hand painted on two sides. The egg splits in half to reveal a simple yellow chicken. These two sets are inexpensive and nice additions to a collection.

Semenov chess and checker sets are made of solid Matreshka figures. Usually the figures are miniatures of the larger sets. The chess and checker pieces display the traditional Semenov characteristics.

All nesting doll collectors must have at least one Semenov set in their collections. It is easily possible to have many Semenov sets in a collection without duplications. New, modern Semenov sets are being imported annually. There are no indications that this region will relinquish its preeminent position among nesting doll producing areas of the U.S.S.R.

Plate 1 18'' set of 24 maidens. The dolls in this very large set of 24 are painted in the traditional Semenov style. The largest doll is 18'' tall. The black-haired maidens have large black eyes and red lips. They wear yellow babushkas with black fingerprint swirl decorations and red dresses. The aprons are painted with various flowers in shades of red, yellow and blue. $800-1000

Plate 2 9'' set of 14 maidens. The traditional dolls in this 9'' set of 14 maidens have some color variations. Most of the dolls are dressed in red dresses, yet two dolls wear deep purple. Every maiden wears a yellow babushka with black fingerprint swirls. They carry bouquets of red, pink and purple flowers. $225-250

Plate 3 Maiden bowling set. This unusual set is about 9'' tall with a large bowling set inside. The traditional maiden wears a red dress and yellow babushka. Her bouquet is painted with red, dark pink and purple flowers. The 8 skinny, solid pins are traditional Semenov maidens. The kingpin is a solid male doll wearing a red cap, yellow shirt and purple trousers. Both balls are solid wood – one red and the other purple.
$50-75

Plate 4 Maiden counting set. This 5½'' set of 11 dolls is unique. The large hollow doll is a traditional Semenov maiden dressed in yellow and red. No shading is used to depict her single red flower. The small counting dolls are solid. They are all dressed in the same clothing as the large doll.
$20-25

Plate 5 52 solid maidens. All 52 dolls in this set are solid wood, painted in the traditional style. The two large dolls stand 3'' and the 50 small dolls are only 1¾''. One large doll is dressed in purple and the other in red. They both wear yellow babushkas with black fingerprint swirls. The 50 small dolls wear yellow babushkas, red dresses and carry red flowers. The set is packaged in a cardboard box like sardines. Rare
$100-150

Plate 6 Box lid of 52 maidens. The box lid of the 52 maiden set is silkscreened in five solid colors – white, yellow, red, green and black. The Russian writing is bright red.

Plate 7 Chef counting set. The 11 piece chef counting set is 6″ tall. The chef is painted very simply. He wears a white chef's hat and blue clothing with a large red flower and greenery. His hair and mustache are painted black and his large eyes are blue. Inside, the small solid chefs are painted in a similar way. Half of the men wear red and the other half wear the same blue as the large chef. $20-25

Plate 8 Cat counting set. This set of 11 male cats is 6″ tall. All 11 cats have green eyes, red noses and black whiskers. They wear red caps. The large cat is dressed in black pants and a red jacket. His natural wood shirt is painted with one large red flower and greenery. The 10 small, solid cats wear black pants, yellow shirts and red bow ties. $20-25

9

Plate 9 Box lid of Cat counting set. The box lid of the Cat counting set is silkscreened in five colors – white, black, red, green and pale orange. The Russian writing is rendered in bright red.

Plate 10 Chicken (Toy) counting set. Mama hen and her baby chicks are a set of 11. The 6″ hen has yellow wings and wears a yellow babushka both with black fingerprint swirls. Her dress and single flower are red. She has red eyes and a protruding beak. The 10 chicks are yellow with red eyes and red flowers on their breasts. $20-25

10

Plate 11 Box lid of Chicken counting set. The cardboard box lid of this chicken counting set is silkscreened in four colors – white, yellow, red and green. The Russian writing is bright red.

Plate 12 14″ Maiden bottle holder I. This beautiful maiden bottle holder is made to open at the bottom. She is 14″ tall and holds a bottle of wine or vodka. She is dressed in traditional Semenov garb – red dress and yellow babushka with black fingerprint swirls. Her bouquet is painted with red and yellow roses. $40-45

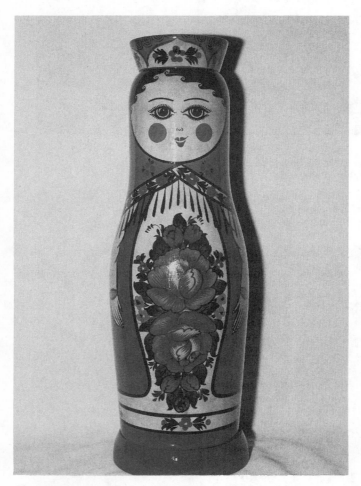

Plate 13 14″ Maiden bottle holder II. This 14″ lovely maiden splits at the bottom to contain a wine or vodka bottle. Her slender body is very detailed. She wears a yellow babushka trimmed with black fringe. Her head is covered with a yellow crown decorated with black fingerprint swirls and red flowers. She wears a red vest and dress. Lovely red roses are painted down her front. $40-45

Plate 14 14″ Male bottle holder I. This 14″ male splits in half to hold a vodka or wine bottle. He wears a large red cap, black trousers and natural wood shirt. He holds a bouquet of red poppies and blue flowers. $40-45

Plate 15 14" Male bottle holder II. This unique male bottle holder splits at the bottom to contain a favorite bottle of spirits. He has black hair and a black mustache. His cap is red with a yellow front and red flower. The black bill of the cap matches his black trousers. His natural wood shirt is trimmed with bands of red flowers and greenery. His bouquet consists of red and yellow roses. $40-45

Plate 16 8" Maiden and male bottle holders. Both of these 8" bottle holders greatly resemble the larger bottle sets. The two dolls split in half. They are dressed in traditional Semenov colors – red, yellow and black. The male has orange hair and a red belt. Both dolls are painted with bright roses of red, pink, yellow and orange. $18-25 each

Plate 17 Warriors and Good Family Man. (Left) The Good Family Man set of four is 5" tall. The white-bearded father is dressed in a yellow coat, and red cap trimmed with fingerprinted fur. The mother is a traditional Semenov maiden dressed in a yellow babushka and red dress. The son's red cap and purple trousers accent his natural wood shirt.

The tiny daughter is garbed in a red cap and skirt and a natural wood coat. (Right) This set of 5 warriors is 6½" tall. All five wear onion domed, red helmets, purple trousers and yellow tunics with black fingerprint swirls. They have white beards and black eyes. The largest warrior carries a yellow club and red shield. $12-18

Plate 18 Egg maidens. This small set of three black-haired maidens is only 3'' tall. The natural wood dolls are decorated with black fingerprint swirls. Large red bows are tied beneath their necks. The smallest doll is dressed in yellow. $7-10

Plate 19 Chicken in egg. The chicken in this 3'' egg is painted yellow with black dot eyes. The natural egg is decorated with black fingerprint swirls and red flowers and greenery. $5-7

Plate 20 Male chess or checker pieces. All chess or checker pieces are made of solid wood. They are smaller versions of other Semenov dolls. These two male chess pieces are painted yellow, red and white.

$50-75 set

POLKHOV MAIDAN

The Polkhov Maidan Matreshka dolls are made in the village of Polkhov Maidan, also in the Gorky region (Voznesen District), east of Moscow. The village (renamed Gorky in modern times) lies near Semenov. The Polkhov Maidan Matreshka dolls are similar to the Semenov maidens, but are taller and thinner. The Polkhov Maidan dolls are painted with water-soluable aniline dyes and black india ink, as compared to the oil paint of the Semenov's. The Polkh dolls lack the high lacquer luster of the Semenov dolls as well. The styles are so similar because of the close proximilty of their villages. In fact, the style of the dolls traveled first from the village of Zagorsk to Semenov and then to Polkhov Maidan.

Before the 1930's, Polkhov Maidan Matreshka dolls were painted without priming the wood. About this time, the craftsmen began to prime the wood with starch and finish them with several layers of clear lacquer. Some people consider the painting and drawing on the Polkhov Maidan dolls naive and childlike. The earlier Polkhov Maidan dolls rendered lines with a red hot needle instead of the contemporary india ink lines. The lines on Polkhov Maidan dolls are important and energetic. The colors are solid and never shaded. The color schemes used include red, yellow, green, turquoise and navy blue.

The Polkhov craftsmen borrowed their painting techniques from the Semenov neighbors, also in the Gorky region. Yet they evolved and developed their own, unique, identifiable style. Lathe turning is the job of the men in the Polkhov Maidan village, while the women paint the dolls. In some ways it can be said that the Polkhov Maidan dolls are the most feminine of all the Matreshka dolls. Perhaps it is due to the female painters.

The Polkhov Maidan dolls have solid, black eyes and lashes with black line eyebrows. Very often the nesting Polkhov Maidan dolls have curly black hair rendered in black ink. Other Polkhov Maidan dolls have blonde, brown, black and orange hair. The face is much smaller than the Semenov faces with pink lips and cheeks. Sometimes the smaller, interior Polkhov Maidan have facial features painted only in black ink. Polkhov Maidan dolls are made with natural wood faces and usually no arms. If arms are drawn, they are sometimes folded.

The Polkhov Maidan dolls wear red dresses with natural wood aprons. The apron or front area is decorated with bright, big flowers in hues of red, yellow and blue. Red and yellow apples and dark green leaves often complete the bouquets. Polkhov Maidan dolls wear yellow shawls with black or red ''fingerprints'' over their heads and shoulders. Variations of red and black shawls are less commonly found. At the forefront of the shawl or cap is always a three-petaled, blue centered flower. The three petals are always two toned, pink and yellow. This is the most distinctive identifying feature of the Polkhov Maidan dolls.

Polkhov Maidan Matreshka dolls are made in several sizes – 1, 2, 3, 4, 5, 6 and 8 in the set. The author has never seen a larger Polkhov Maidan set than eight. The author has likewise only seen one Polkhov Maidan Matreshka Man. He is photographed on Plate 94 in *Russian Folk Style Figurines* by Gennady Blinov. There are two lovely variations of the maiden dolls. These sets of three maidens have tall, thin bodies with small heads, and full skirts. They wear the identifying caps with the three petaled, blue centered flower. In addition, the maidens have arms drawn on and carry baskets.

Other Polkhov Maidan Matreshka sets include Polkh babies, a small, sewing girl, a single, solid girl with a full skirt, Polkhov Maidan lady boxes and a Czarinka box. The sewing kit is a single, hollow maiden with blonde hair. Inside is a lathe turned piece of wood that holds thread and needles. The solid single girl with a full skirt has black hair and a removeable head. The Polkhov Maidan lady boxes and the Czarinka box are single, large, hollow dolls. They are rendered in great detail with many lovely colors. They have unusual shapes for Matreshka dolls. The lady box has the curly, black hair of the nested dolls. The Czarinka box has a separate head and crown. She has orange-blonde hair. Her neck functions as an egg holder. As the Czar's wife, she is very noble in her posture. These two boxes are beautiful, but difficult to locate.

The Polkhov Maidan dolls are close in design to the Semenov dolls, yet a few characteristics help identify the differences. The Polkhov Maidan dolls do not wear babushkas, but yellow shawls or caps over their heads and shoulders. The shawl or cap is always attached to a three petaled, blue centered flower. The Polkhov Maidan dolls have solid black eyes and eyelashes. Most often, they have no arms. The primary hairstyle is rendered in black curly lines. However, black, brown, blonde and orange hair are occasionally found. The bouquets often include red and yellow apples and blue flowers. The Polkhov Maidan dolls have small heads, sometimes separated from the bodies, and tall, thin figures. All collectors should compare and contrast the characteristics of the Semenov and Polkhov Maidan sets.

Plate 21 10¾'' set of 8 maidens. This lovely set of 10 dolls is 10¾'' tall. The Polkh design of black curly hair is rendered on all the dolls. They wear the traditional Polkh flower with a blue center and three petals of red and yellow. Their yellow veils are decorated with black fingerprint swirls. The armless dolls wear red dresses with bouquets of red, white, purple, yellow and pink flowers. $70-80

Plate 22 Yellow veil set of 5 maidens. This 6'' set of five dolls is typical of Polkh dolls. All five have black curly hair and black facial features. They are dressed with the Polkh flower on their yellow veils. Their red dresses are without arms. The dolls have bouquets of simple pink, red, turquoise and yellow flowers. The smallest doll is dressed in yellow. $20-25

Plate 23 Red veil set of five maidens. This 6'' set of five maidens is unusual for several reasons. The largest doll in this set has brown curly hair. Lovely long eyelashes have been drawn on the eyes of these maidens. The veils of the largest two dolls are red. They wear the traditional Polkh flower, red dresses and no arms. The bouquets consist of red and pink poppies, and red and yellow buds. The smallest doll is dressed in yellow. $20-25

Plate 24 Black veil set of five maidens. The 6″ set of five dolls is unique because the largest doll wears a black veil. In other ways, the set is typical of the Polkh maidens – red dresses, yellow flowers and black curly hair.
$25-35

Plate 25 Mini set of two maidens. This miniature set of two is only 2″ tall. The typical Polkh maidens have curly black hair, red dresses, yellow veils and polkh flowers. Their bouquets are simple flowers of red and yellow.
$5-7

Plate 26 Thin maidens with baskets. The three dolls in this 6⅛″ set have a most unusual shape. The curly-haired dolls wear yellow bonnets with a Polkh flower, red and turquoise dresses and natural wood pinafores. Simple flowers of red, pink, yellow and blue decorate the dolls. These dolls are unusual for Polkh maidens because they have arms. Each maiden carries a yellow basket.
$17-20

Plate 27 Polkh babies. The darling Polkh babies in these two sets of three are 3¾'' tall. The curly-haired dolls wear red dresses and yellow veils with the Polkh flower. They hold their arms crossed across their chests. The dolls are completed with bouquets of red, pink and yellow flowers. $10-15

Plate 28 Maiden variations. The three sets of dolls are variations of the Polkh maidens. The largest doll is 6½'' tall. They are painted in many colors – red, yellow, purple, green, pink and turquoise. $15-25

Plate 29 Solid maidens. Each of these single dolls is a different set. They are 3¼-3¾'' tall. (Left) This beautiful doll has a full skirt and a removeable head. She is painted in lovely shades of red, turquoise and natural wood tones. (Middle) The doll in the middle splits in half to reveal a sewing kit. She is a blonde with a yellow cap. Her clothing is painted in shades of red, black and natural woods tones. (Right) This solid doll is typical of Polkh maidens with her yellow veil, red dress and simple bouquet. $5-10

Plate 30 Maiden and Czarinka Boxes. All three of these gorgeous dolls split in half to hold treasures. They are 7½-9'' tall. All three wear very detailed clothing in shades of yellow, red, purple, pink, turquoise and black. $25-40

17

ZAGORSK

The Moscow region is located a few miles northeast of Moscow in the modern town of Zagorsk. Originally, Zagorsk was the settlement of Sergiev Posad and the Troitse-Sergeyev Monastery. As early as the fifteenth century, the Monastery village existed as a large wood carving center and toy producer. More recently, it was the Sergiev Posad (Zagorsk) woodcarvers who first quickly imitated the original Malyutin Matreshkas. The Zagorsk Matreshka style traveled from Zagorsk to Semenov and on to Polkhov Maidan in the early part of this century.

Today in Zagorsk a Soviet co-operative exists. Craftsmen work in a factory where only Matreshkas are made. The labor is divided and the dolls are made in an assembly-line fashion. The craftsmen use modern themes as well as traditional ones. Zagorsk is the home of a large toy museum, and Russia's only school to train toymakers. Nearly a million Matreshka sets a year are manufactured for the world market in Zagorsk.

Some of the very earliest examples of Zagorsk sets were unpainted and unvarnished. The designs were instead delineated with poker work, also known as wood burning. Early examples of these sets are occasionally found here in the United States. The sets are almost never complete, as pieces are lost over time.

The early Zagorsk sets included boys and men within the maiden sets. Today they are rarely included. The boys usually have brown hair and wear shirts of yellow, blue or pink with red belts tied around their waists.

The Zagorsk maidens have been called the humblest doll style. While these Matreshkas are gentle and poetic in appearance, they may be regarded as the least artistic of the Russian nesting dolls. Less detail is evident in the designs, the colors are more muted, and in some instances, the workmanship can be rather crude. The wood itself is thicker, contributing to a less delicate overall appearance and feel.

The head takes up nearly a third of the total doll. The face itself is almost square shaped with rounded edges. The Zagorsk dolls are the only Matreshkas that are completely painted including the flesh tones of the face and hands. Their cheeks are quite pale in comparison to their Semenov sisters. The eyes, nose and brows are usually rendered in dark brown or black ink. The eyes are a mere large dot inside arches. Zagorsk dolls have tiny, red, heart-shaped mouths. Light brown hair is a unique identifying feature, although smaller dolls within a set and older dolls occasionally have black hair. Dolls from this region are painted with gouache (opaque water colors) and coated with a low gloss varnish.

Zagorsk Matreshka maidens wear babushkas in simple colors of red, green, blue, orange and yellow. The babushkas may be decorated with flowers and greenery. In some sets, they are simple and unadorned. The Zagorsk maidens wear sarafans with straps, a long sleeved blouse and an apron. The apron is tied up under the armpits. This peasant fashion is very appealing. The Zagorsk maidens are one of the few Matreshkas that do not carry a bouquet of flowers. In larger sets, the maidens sometimes carry baskets of fruit or tied kerchief purses in their hands. Simple "dot" flowers often adorn their aprons. Simple sets from Zagorsk generally eliminate arms and aprons.

Zagorsk maidens are made in sets of 3, 4, 5, 6, 7, 8, 11, 12 and more. There are two basic types of maidens. One is simple in style with virtually no decorations, aprons or arms. The second type of set is much more detailed with flowers on the aprons and babushkas. She is drawn with arms, one up and the other at her side. The detailed sets are more closely nested. They have been referred to as mini-nested. The Zagorsk craftsmen make a maiden box. She is basically a hollow, single, detailed Zagorsk Matreshka.

Modern sets of Ice Hockey teams, Ship's crews, Farm workers and Cosmonauts are mentioned by Ann Bahar in her *Doll Reader* article, "Matreoschka" (Dec. 1984/Jan. 1985). However, the author has never seen these Zagorsk sets here in the U.S.A. As mentioned before, almost no males are ever included in maiden sets today. It is possible to find old Zagorsk sets that do include boys, as Zagorsk and Semenov sets were the first to be imported to the U.S. What the Zagorsk dolls lack in flair is made up for in simplicity of charm and honesty. A humble Zagorsk Matreshka is a definite must for the collector.

Plate 31 Old unpainted maidens (2). This is an example of a very early set. The two maidens are unpainted with wood burned features. The wood has been left in its natural state – unstained and unvarnished. There were originally more pieces in this set. These early sets are most difficult to locate today. Rare $50-100

Plate 32 Old family set with boys (6). This early 6¼'' set of 6 Zagorsk dolls includes three boys. Each brown-haired doll has a handpainted face with simple black features. The women wear babushkas, while the boys are without hats. The boys' clothing is painted yellow, green or red with red string belts. The largest boy wears green mittens. The women are dressed in babushkas, sarafans with straps, long sleeved blouses and aprons. The women's clothing is painted dark blue, yellow, red and orange. The largest lady has simple dot flowers decorating her apron. She carries a brown kerchief bag as well. Like most Zagorsk dolls, they do not carry bouquets. Rare $50-125

Plate 33 Old set of three maidens. This 4'' set of three is quite old. The three maidens have painted faces, black facial features and dark brown hair. They are dressed in clothing painted red, yellow and green. These simple dolls carry no bouquets. Rare $25-50

19

Plate 34 Old sets with male dolls. These early sets of Zagorsk dolls included boys. The sets are 4-5¼'' tall. Every doll has a handpainted face with simple black features. The women wear babushkas, while the boys are bareheaded. The boys' simple clothing is painted either yellow or pink with red string belts. The women are dressed in dark blues, greens, yellows and red. These typical Zagorsk dolls do not carry bouquets. Rare $25-50

Plate 35 Modern sets of maidens. (Left) The four dolls in this 5'' set are typical Zagorsk maidens. They have brown hair and handpainted faces. Their simple clothes are painted red, yellow, green and blue. (Middle) This 4'' set of six is sometimes called mini-nested. The brown-haired maidens are painted with more detail. The colors used are white, yellow, blue, red, green, brown and orange (Right) This 3½'' set of three is the most simple Zagorsk set made. The dolls are painted in yellow, red, green and orange clothing. $10-26 maiden.

KIROV

The Kirov region is located northwest of Semenov and quite a distance northwest from Moscow. Like their Semenov sisters, the Kirov maidens are very brightly painted. Kirov dolls also have broad bodies with proportionately large heads. The Kirov dolls closely resemble the Semenov sets with two major exceptions. The Kirov Matreshkas always have orange "carrot color" hair and large, solid black eyes. Often, larger dolls in Kirov sets have eyelashes. A Semenov's eyebrows curve to complement the eyes. The Kirov brows are rendered as a straight line above the eye. Another difference occurs in the style of the mouth. Kirov dolls have smaller red mouths with a thin, black line separating the lips.

The Kirov dolls wear babushkas of yellow, red or purple. On occasion, the babushkas are left a natural wood tone with colored polka dots all over the scarf. Sometimes the babushkas are decorated with red, white or black "fingerprint" swirl designs. The Kirov dresses are painted dark, deep purples, yellow and natural wood with polka dots. The author has rarely seen a Kirov maiden with a red dress, the typical color of a Semenov doll.

The aprons vary in style and design on Kirov dolls. The dolls carry simple bouquets of flowers, usually red blooms with greenery. Smaller dolls will carry a blossom or two. Kirov dolls can be decorated with red berries or bunches of red or purple grapes. Like the Semenov dolls, the features of the dolls including aprons, babushkas and arms are rendered in delicate black lines.

The Kirov Matreshkas can be found in sets of 1, 2, 3, 4, 5, 6, 7, 10, 12 and more. A beautiful set of 10 was made to commemorate the 1980 Moscow Olympic games. She is very unique because she has big, blue eyes. Another lovely set of 10 was produced with large, violet eyes. These maidens are unusual because they wear natural wood, flower painted shawls trimmed with fringe. The shawls are draped over their shoulders. The maidens also wear matching mittens. Their dresses are painted yellow, purple or red. A Kirov Matreshka also appears as a musical, roly poly figure. The roly poly is made in the same manner as a typical Matreshka. However, her bottom is rounded, not flat. Inside the heavy, sealed doll are metal bells. When the doll is tipped, the bells jingle and she returns to an upright position. This roly poly is difficult to locate, but a lovely variation.

In recent years, a new development has occurred with Matreshkas from Kirov. Special Kirov maidens are designed with straw or wheat geometric designs inlaid all over the dolls. These dolls have the traditional Kirov shape, faces and hair color. Their clothing is decorated completely with minute, complex geometric patterns of natural wheat. There are two color variations used for the wheat inlaid dolls. Sometimes the sets contain both variations. Dark purple, red and yellow are the primary combinations used on wheat inlaid sets. The second variation combines red, yellow and green. These beautiful inlaid sets are sometimes difficult to locate. They are made in sets of 5, 6, 7, 12 and more. A wheat inlaid version of the musical roly poly is produced. Both roly poly dolls are difficult to locate, but beautiful when found.

If the Kirov region manufactures male Matreshka sets, the author has never seen them. Since there are male Matreshka dolls manufactured in Semenov, Polkhov Maidan, Zagorsk and other Soviet regions, perhaps Kirov males are produced, but not imported into the United States. Male Kirov dolls would be a welcome addition to collections, along with both types of Kirov maidens – the traditional and the lovely, wheat inlaid sets.

Plate 36 5¼" set of seven maidens. These seven typical Kirov maidens stand 5¼" tall. They have orange colored hair and black facial features. Their babushkas are yellow with either black or red fingerprint swirls. The dresses are varied in design and color – purple, yellow and natural wood tone. The bouquest include red flowers and red grapes. $20-30

21

Plate 37 6½'' set of three maidens. These three large dolls have the carrot colored hair and large black eyes. Each doll in the 6½'' set wears a different color dress – purple, yellow and red. Likewise, their babushkas are different – one yellow and the others are natural wood. Their bouquets are bunches of red berries. $10-18

Plate 38 7'' set of 10 maidens. These exceptionally beautiful 10 dolls have bright orange hair and large purple eyes. Their dresses are simple and yellow. They wear natural wood scarves on their heads and wrapped around their necks. Black fringe trims the scarf of the largest doll. Beautiful flowers of red and blue decorate the front and back of the scarves. Flower-painted mittens warm the hands of the largest 7'' maiden. $40-50

Plate 39 1980 Moscow Olympic maidens. The 1980 Moscow Olympics were honored in this 7'' set of 10. The carrot colored hair maidens have large blue eyes. Their babushkas are either yellow or natural wood. Their dresses are painted purple, yellow, red or natural wood. Various flowers in many shades of red and pink decorate the fronts of the dresses. The largest doll has a ribbon across her chest that says ''Moscow 80'' in Russian. Rare $110-120

Plate 40 Small Semenov and Kirov maidens. These two small sets of three and four dolls are 3-4'' tall. The Semenov dolls on the left have black hair, yellow babushkas, red dresses and round aprons. The Kirov dolls on the right have orange hair, yellow dresses, red or natural wood babushkas and square aprons. $7-10

Plate 41 Roly Poly maiden. When you tip the round base of this very heavy 4½″ Kirov roly poly, she makes music. The heavy bells within her chime and tinkle. She has orange hair and large black eyes. Her bouquet consists of red, pink, yellow and turquoise flowers. She wears a red babushka and yellow dress. Her cardboard box is silkscreened in four colors – white, turquoise, red and yellow. $12-25

Plate 42 Wheat inlaid and plain maidens. (Left) There are two dolls missing from this 4″ set of wheat inlaid dolls. The orange haired maidens are decorated with geometric patterns of natural wheat. Their clothing is painted red, yellow, green and purple. (Right) The three dolls in this 3¼″ set are plain Kirov maidens. They have carrot colored hair, yellow dresses and either red or natural wood babushkas. $12-15

Plate 43 Wheat inlaid set of 12 maidens. This lovely 8'' set of 12 dolls is decorated with intricate geometric patterns of natural wheat. They have the traditional orange hair and large black eyes. All their clothing is painted yellow, red and purple. $90-100

Plate 44 Wheat inlaid set of five maidens. This smaller set of five wheat inlaid maidens are 4¼'' tall. The natural wheat designs accent the bright red, yellow and purple clothing. These typical Kirov dolls have black eyes and orange hair. $20-25

KALININ

The Kalinin Matreshka dolls are made in the town of Kalinin on the Upper Volga River, northwest of Moscow. The craft of Matreshka-making is relatively new to the Kalinin village. The dolls have been crafted there for about 60 years. The Kalinin dolls have several variations in design, but can never be confused with the classical Semenov dolls.

The Kalinin dolls have natural wood faces, blouses and hands. They have very happy expressions with bright blue eyes, pink cheeks and red mouths with red line noses. The Kalinin dolls are always blonde or light brown brunettes, never black haired.

The most identifying feature of the Kalinin dolls are the brown, wood burned grooves that define and delineate the geometric patterns. These lines are also called poker work. The Kalinin maidens wear bright babushkas tied beneath their chins in shades of red, orange, yellow, green and blue. Sometimes sets will be made with alternating colors that match their ponevas or jumpers. Their babushkas are simply decorated with polka dot flowers and single polka dots. They wear long sleeved blouses of natural wood tones. Their ponevas are usually plain with a simple geometric design or polka dot flowers. They are painted bright colors – red, orange, green, blue and yellow. Some Kalinin dolls wear polka dot bead necklaces.

The bright Kalinin maidens are made in three sizes – 3, 5 and 6 per set. A thinner set of three maidens is also made. The thin maidens are painted black and red. These dolls are blonde with black babushkas, black beads around their necks, red vests and geometric patterns. A single, tall, pencil box maiden is also produced. She has blonde hair and is dressed in geometric patterns of orange and yellow.

Weighted maiden and male roly poly dolls are made in Kalinin. When you push the doll over, it bounces back. Sometimes the roly poly dolls are made as a single unit. Other times the roly poly is the smallest doll in a nested set.

Modern male Kalinin boxes are made. One male box is a 10.75'' warrior created with great detail. The warrior has various patterns of wood burned lines on his natural wood body. He wears a helmet and carries a spear and shield. Other than roly polys and boxes, the author has never seen a modern male Kalinin nested doll.

In times past, Kalinin nesting warriors were produced. One particular old set is marked, ''Made in the Soviet Union.'' These dark hued warriors wear helmets and tunics of red and yellows. The largest warrior has a full white beard and mustache, while an inside warrior is brunette and clean shaven. Any Kalinin Matreshka adds color to a collection.

Plate 45 Set of six maidens. The six dolls in this 5½'' set have very sunny expressions. The dolls are woodburned to delineate clothing. Each doll has brown hair and blue eyes. They wear babushkas and ponevas in bright colors – red, orange, yellow, green, pink and blue. Simple geometric patterns or dot flowers decorate the ponevases. $18-30

Plate 46 Sets of three, one and five maidens. The blonde dolls in these three sets range in size from 4-4½'' tall. Each maiden has woodburned grooves to delineate her clothing. They are painted in bright colors – red, yellow, green and bright pink. Dot flowers are painted on some of the larger dolls in the sets. $6-18

Plate 47 Three maidens and roly poly maiden. (Left) The three maidens in this 4½'' set are tall and thin. The geometric patterns in their clothing are woodburned lines. They wear clothing of natural wood tones, red and black. (Right) This single roly poly is short and fat at 3'' tall. When you push her over, she wobbles back as a weight is inside her rounded bottom. The blue-eyed blonde is dressed in a green babushka, red dress and pink beads. Her clothing has been delineated with woodburned lines. $9-12

Plate 48 Maiden Box. This lovely single maiden box is 8'' tall. Svetlana, as she is sometimes called, is tall and quite thin. Her blonde hair is covered by an orange babushka. She has bright blue eyes and a happy expression. Her clothing is painted red, yellow and orange. The geometric patterns are made with woodburning. $18-25

Plate 49 Male warrior box. This tall, thin, single warrior box is 10'' tall. Many additional pieces of wood have been added to make him quite elaborate. (His orange and natural wood helmet, natural wood nose, hand and spear and his woodburned, round shield are separate pieces glued on.) Many details have been woodburned. He has brown eyes, hair and a long brown beard. His clothing is primarily natural wood with a panel down the front. The panel is made of woodburned geometric patterns and painted red and orange. $18-22

Plate 50 Male old warriors. This 3¼'' set of two is quite old. At one time, there was at least one more piece. The woodburned men wear helmets and mail painted in shades of rose, brown and gold. The largest man wears a white beard and his companion is a clean shaven brunette. Rare $25-35

Plate 51 Male roly poly. This single male roly poly is about 3'' tall. When you push his rounded bottom, he bounces back. He is weighted and heavy. This blue-eyed brunette is primarily natural wood with woodburned accents. His collar is painted red, and blue dots cover his shirt. He plays a balalaika. $10-15

BREST REGION

The Brest region, also known as White Russia or Belorussia is a major production center for Matreshkas. The Brest region encompasses all of White Russia and is located north of the Ukraine, due west of Moscow, south of Leningrad and east of Poland, Lithuania and Latvia.

The Brest region is very prolific. They manufacture at least twenty-one different Matreshka sets including maidens, men and animals. The region has produced a variety of themes not readily found elsewhere in the U.S.S.R. Some modern examples include Father Frost and Cosmonauts.

The Brest region sets tend to be smaller than those of the other regions. Seven appears to be the largest set. The characteristics that identify Brest dolls include high gloss and smooth finishes. Often the dolls have pointed heads. The dolls always have natural wood faces and blue eyes. The clothing is usually painted in muted tones – greens, oranges, reds, dark blues, browns, greys and blacks. Some Brest sets are painted in pastel colors and whites.

There are eight distinct maiden types. The maidens have blonde, red and brown hair. The Brest Nina is a set of seven red-haired maidens. They wear red babushkas, natural wood blouses, dark green vests, dark blue skirts and natural wood aprons. A second maiden type is the Black Lacquered Maidens. They are made in sets of 5, 6 and 7. The brown-haired maidens wear black lacquered dresses with red water lilies and greenery on the front. An earlier version has orange water lilies instead. Their babushkas alternate in a set between dark red and green. The Brest Vitka maidens are a third distinct type of Brest maidens. The Vitkas are produced in sets of 4, 5, 6 and 7. Their heart shaped faces, red hair and crossed arms are quite unique. There are two different Pastel maidens. One set is made with vests and skirts in alternating pastel colors. The other pastel maidens are made in sets of 5, 6 and 7. The blondes wear white aprons, natural wood shawls, green plaid skirts and pastel babushkas of red, pink, green and blue. The Christmas maidens, a sixth type, are very similar to the pastel maidens. The blondes are dressed in natural wood aprons, dark green plaid skirts, green shawls and red babushkas. The Christmas dolls are made in sets of 5, 6 and 7. The seventh and eighth types of maidens are small. The four dolls in one set have blonde hair. Two color variations are manufactured, one with green vest and pink water lilies on her apron. The other wears a blue vest with red water lily on the apron. A set of three maidens is similar to this set. They wear a green vest, green skirt and natural wood blouse. Single box and solid Matreshkas in various sizes and styles are also Brest products. These single sets include maidens, heroes and a red-haired man called, ''Smurfski.''

More sets of men are made in the Brest region than anywhere else in the U.S.S.R. With the exception of the Cosmonauts, the Brest men are always bearded. The fisherman is a single box. He is red-haired and bearded, holding a large orange fish and net. The woodcutters are similar to the fishermen. The five red-headed men hold various tools in their hands. Each tool is different, including axe, saw, hammer and chisels. The woodcutters wear natural wood shirts and striped trousers in hues of orange and grey. The gnomes, sometimes called the seven dwarfs, wear dark muted clothing and red caps, belts and shoes. Each white bearded gnome carries a mining tool. The largest gnome holds a bag of jewels. A new set variation of the gnomes consists of seven, smiling, grey bearded men holding mushrooms and berries. They are dressed in brighter colors and polka dots. Father Frost (Santa Claus) is a lovely new set of four introduced in the U.S. in 1986. The grey bearded gentlemen wear fur accented coats and caps in soft shades of red, blue and green. Their coats are decoated with white snowflakes. The largest Father Frost carries a tall staff topped with a snowflake and holds a green Christmas tree. Other Father Frosts hold bags of goodies and Christmas letters. All four gentlemen wear warm mittens. Two sets of Heroes have been manufactured. An earlier version of three red or yellow bearded warriors carried blue shields and grey spears. A newer set of three, brown bearded heroes became available in 1986. These warriors wear orange mail, red capes, grey helmets, grey shields and hold grey swords. It is next to impossible to locate the red or blond bearded heroes now. Finally, the modern Cosmonauts are a brand new set of four from the Brest region. They are ready for space travel in their spacesuits of orange and royal blue with alternating helmet colors. Quite humorous are these spacemen.

Recently two Brest animal sets of four were imported. Blue and white penguins with red beaks and feet delight collectors. They appear very cool from arctic regions. A wise set of orange and green owls have also flown in to American collections. Possibly more animal sets will follow.

Brest chess and checker sets are made of solid Matreshka figures. Usually they are miniatures of larger Brest nested dolls. The chess and checker pieces display the same characteristics known to all Brest dolls.

The Brest region artists are very creative in the themes they choose for their nesting doll sets. The author fully expects many more unique sets to be manufactured in this delightful region.

Plate 52 Brest Nina maidens. The seven-piece Nina set is 5½'' tall. The orange haired maidens have blue eyes. Their rounded red babushkas are decorated with two blue lines at the hem. They wear dark green vests with orange bands. The dark blue plaid skirts have brown lines. The natural wood blouses and aprons are trimmed with geometric patterns of red, orange and black. $35-40

Plate 53 Black Lacquered maidens I. The six dolls in this 4½'' set have pointed heads. They have brown hair and big blue eyes. The dolls wear red or green babushkas decorated with brown. Their dresses are either green or red in an alternating color pattern. The front panels are black with two red water lilies and greenery. $22-28

30

Plate 54 Black Lacquered maidens II. The five dolls in this set are 3½'' tall. They have pointed heads, brown hair and blue eyes. The red or muted green babushkas are decorated with brown. The dresses are painted either red or green in an alternating sequence. The orange water lilies with pale green leaves decorate their black front panels. $16-20

Plate 55 Brest Vitka maidens. In this 3½'' set of five, the dolls have rounded heads and crossed arms. There is a space of flesh between their orange hair and babushkas. The maidens have large blue eyes and red dot lips. They wear black vests, natural wood blouses and aprons trimmed in red. Each doll's plaid skirt or fringed babushka is a different dark color – blue, green, orange or red. $22-28

Plate 56 Pastel maiden set of five with vests. All five blondes in this 4'' set have round heads. They wear babushkas, vests and skirts in an alternating color pattern. The blouses and vests are white with red geometric trim. The vests, babushkas and skirts are red, pale blue or pale green. $10-20

Plate 57 Pastel maidens. The seven blondes in this 5½'' set have rounded heads and blue eyes. They wear white blouses and aprons with red and black accents. Their skirts are natural wood and green plaid. They wear natural wood shawls which have curved edges and are decorated with flowers. Each babushka is a pastel color – either red, pink, pale blue or pale green. $35-40

32

Plate 58 Christmas maidens. All seven dolls are dressed alike in this 5½'' set. The orange-haired dolls have rounded heads and big blue eyes. The blouses and aprons are natural wood with red and black trim. The maidens wear red babushkas, dark green curved vests and green and natural wood plaid skirts. $35-40

Plate 59 Set of four maidens. The four maidens in this 4½'' set have blonde hair, blue eyes and pointed heads. They are all dressed alike in red babushkas with yellow polka dots. The dolls wear red, short sleeved blouses, blue vests with red polka dots and orange skirts. Their natural wood aprons are decorated with single red water lilies and greenery. $19-25

Plate 60 Set of three maidens. All three dolls in this 4½'' set have pointed heads, blonde hair and blue eyes. They wear identical clothing with red babushkas decorated with white dots. Each maiden wears a natural wood blouse trimmed in red and a natural wood apron. Their vests and skirts are green with pale green and brown stripes. $12-15

Plate 61 Solid maidens. These three blonde, blue-eyed, solid maidens range in size from 2-4'' The three dolls wear red babushkas trimmed in brown or orange. The largest doll is dressed in a natural wood vest and apron with red and black trim. Her vest has orange and her skirt is green, grey and blue stripes. She holds a single red flower in her hands. The two small dolls have natural wood dresses with round black aprons. The aprons are decorated with red water lilies. The smallest doll is a Christmas tree ornament. $3-8

Plate 62 Solid men. The four solid men range in size from 2-4¼'' tall. The tallest man is a redheaded king, dressed in red, yellow and natural wood. The redheaded Smurfsky is dressed in an orange tam, green jacket and natural wood trousers. The grey-bearded man wears a multi-stripped tam, red tie, grey trousers and natural wood shirt. The small, red-haired viking wears a yellow helmet and grey tunic. He holds a blue sword and red shield. $3-8

Plate 63 Fisherman box and Woodcutters. (Left) The fisherman is a single, round headed box. He stands 6¾'' tall as one of the largest Brest pieces. The balding man has orange hair, a beard and mustache. He is dressed in a natural wood shirt with red and black geometric trim. He wears a brown vest with a blue band and blue trousers. He holds a large orange fish and a black fishing net. (Right) The 5½'' set of wood-cutters has pointed heads. The blue-eyed men have orange hair, beards and mustaches. They wear natural wood shirts trimmed with geometric bands of red and black patterns. Each man wears grey and yellow striped trousers. They hold various tools painted brown and grey. $12-24

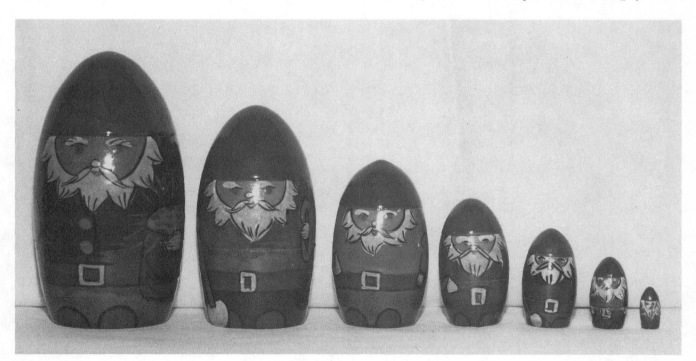

Plate 64 Gnomes. This set, also known as the seven dwarfs, is 4¾'' tall. The dwarfs wear red stocking caps with a groove at their base. Each blue-eyed dwarf has a short white beard and white nose. They all wear red belts and shoes and blue pants. The shirts are painted different colors – green, blue, yellow, brown and orange. Every dwarf carries a different mining tool including picks, shovels, chisels, rope and a large bag of jewels. $25-35

Plate 65 Gnomes II. These seven, happy, smiling gnomes are 4½'' tall. They are blue-eyed with long white beards and large noses. Each gnome wears a red stocking cap and brown shoes. Their shirts are natural wood with various designs – polka dots, plaid, stars and crosses in assorted colors. They each wear a different color of pants – dark green, turquoise, orange, blue and light green. The gnomes hold various natural items – mushrooms, pinecones, acorns, berries and flowers. $25-35

Plate 66 Father Frost. This 4½'' Father Frost is a Russian variation of Santa Claus. The four Father Frosts have large blue eyes and long grey beards. Each Father Frost wears a white fur trimmed cap and coat. The caps and coats are red, green or pale blue with white snowflakes. The dolls wear mittens of red, green or pale blue. The largest man holds a green Christmas tree and a blue staff topped with an ice crystal. The second man holds a large red sack, while the third carries a letter. $19-25

Plate 67 Heroes (2 versions). (Left) This set of three Heroes is the older version. The men stand 5½'' tall with orange hair, eyebrows, mustaches and beards. They wear pointed helmets of grey, brown and orange. All three men wear red capes, natural wood trousers and brown mail. They carry spears of grey and shields of dark blue. (Right) This smaller set of three brown-bearded heroes is a newer version. The men are 4½'' with grey and blue pointed helmets. They wear mail of orange and blue, grey shirts and red capes. They hold swords and shields of grey. $12-18

Plate 68 Cosmonauts. The cosmonaut set of four represents a modern theme in nesting dolls. The men stand 4¼'' tall with rounded heads. They wear space helmets and suits, gloves and boots in either turquoise or orange in alternating colors. The suits are decorated with red insignia and brown or blue bands. $14-18

Plate 69 Penguins. This frosty set of four are 4½'' tall with pointed heads. They are all alike with red beaks, feet and a few red feathers on their heads. They have white breasts and faces with blue eyes. The heads, wings and backs are light and dark blue. $14-18

Plate 70 Owls. These pointed head owls are 4½'' tall. All four are alike with light orange beaks and eyebrows. They see with large green eyes. The heads and backs are painted orange. The wings, breasts and tails are all natural wood with feathers of orange, brown, green and light orange. $14-18

Plate 71 Chess pieces. Chess and checker pieces from the Brest region include both male and female dolls. The dolls are miniature version of larger nesting sets. They range in size from 4¼''-2'' tall. The solid figures are either blonde or orange-haired. The kings, rooks, etc. are dressed in various colors of red, yellow, black and grey. $50-65/chess set

THE UKRAINE

The Ukraine is a Union Republic of the Soviet Union. This Slavic country is located southwest of Russian, north of Moldavia, south of White Russia and west of Poland. It is the third largest republic in the Soviet system. Like Moldavia, it too, once was an independent country. The Ukrainians are slavic people, similar in ethnicity to the Russians.

The Ukraine produces at least thirteen different Matreshka sets. The typical colorations of Ukrainian dolls include red and yellow combinations. Browns, oranges, greens and blues are also used. The tones of the clothing on these dolls are often dark and muted. Detailed geometric patterns are frequently used.

The Ukrainian dolls have natural wood faces and hands. The hair coloring is usually dark brown or black. However, some orange haired dolls can be found. Most Ukrainian dolls have black eyes, brows and noses with red mouths. Pink cheeks are absent from the faces of the Ukrainian dolls.

Two Ukrainian sets are produced with unusual lathe patterns. The dolls in these sets have small heads with almost normal body proportions. One set contains three male figures, while the other is composed of three female figures. The dolls are painted in dark browns, tans and orange variations. Much natural wood has been left exposed. Geometric patterns of great detail decorate the dolls.

Small, thin bullet shaped Ukrainian Matreshka maidens can be found in sets of three, four, eight and nine. The dolls, called Gutsulka maidens, are one simple shape with white blouses, dark vests and babushkas. They are usually painted with browns, tans, oranges and greens. They, too, have greatly detailed geometric patterns as well as floral designs. The larger sets with eight or nine dolls carry large bouquets of flowers. A unique variation of this doll is manufactured. This set of four dolls has unusual facial features of closed eyes and open mouths. The author has never seen any other Russian dolls with these distinctive characteristics. Their expression suggests they are singing. Perhaps they are praying, yawning or sleeping. At any rate, they are very lovely. Similar sets of maidens are made in a conical shape. These maidens are made in sets of three, five, six and nine. The tiny set of three carries a large bouquet of red flowers. The set of five carries a book in her arms. The largest doll in the set of six holds a swaddled baby in her arms. The baby is wrapped in pink. The largest set of nine conical shaped dolls holds a loaf of bread and salt. These eight sets are all lovely and quite detailed.

Two less detailed sets are made. The first set wears the common Ukrainian red and yellow combinations. The dolls wear red babushkas and a yellow dress accented with red and black. They place their hands inside red pockets. On their back is a large black area with geometric colors. A red-haired set of four is made wearing long red babushkas and navy blue dresses. The dolls welcome you with a fresh loaf of bread and a long towel, slavic symbols of hospitality.

Ukrainian Easter eggs (Pysanky) are well known all over the world. Usually real chicken, duck or goose eggs are blown clean and decorated on the surface. Pysanky making is a very time consuming process. The pysanky are made in several steps using wax, colored dyes, and kistky (writing tools). Two sets of wooden nesting eggs are made in the Ukraine to resemble the pysanky. The first set of three is made with mother-of-pearl inlay and geometric patterns. The second set of three wooden eggs is hand painted in typical Ukrainian style. Geometric patterns of reds, yellows, oranges and blacks are hand painted and then highly lacquered. These nesting eggs are found in the spring.

Sets of three or four dolls are the most common Ukrainian sizes. Sets of nine dolls are the largest Ukrainian sets the author has seen. Ukrainian dolls and wooden nesting eggs are not readily available in the United States. When located, they add a new flavor to a collection. The detailed geometric patterns are stimulating to the eye and highly distinctive.

Plate 72 Male and maidens sets of three. The lovely sets of three are made in unusual shapes. The sets are 6¼'' tall. They are painted with detailed geometric designs. All the dolls have brown hair. Much natural wood has been left. The geometric patterns are painted in earth tones of dark and light brown, black, orange and yellow. The largest man holds a brown flute. $20-25/set

41

Plate 73 Bullet and conical maidens. These two sets of three represent the two most common Ukrainian doll shapes. (Left) The three dolls in this 3¼'' set are bullet-shaped. Each doll has a different hair color – brown, black and tan. They wear very intricate geometric patterns on their blouses, babushkas, aprons and skirts. The largest doll has two yellow birds painted on the back of her babushka. Colors used are black, brown, tan, yellow, orange, green and maroon. (Right) The three dolls in this 2¾'' set are conical or egg-shaped. They have either black or brown hair. The dolls wear white blouses with orange and red patterns. Their vests are black or dark brown. They wear striped skirts of green or red. Very elaborate floral patterns are painted on their yellow and green babushkas. The largest doll has a brown bird painted on the back of her scarf. She also carries a large bouquet of red flowers. The middle doll carries a book. $14-20

Plate 74 Singing maidens. This 4'', bullet-shaped set of four dolls is most unusual. The dolls have their eyes closed and their mouths open as if they were singing. They have their arms folded over their chests. The black-haired dolls wear either green or orange babushkas, black or brown vests, and skirts of green or orange. Intricate patterns are painted on their white blouses. Elaborate floral patterns decorate their babushkas. $15-20

Plate 75 Set of nine Bullet maidens. This very large set of nine bullet-shaped maidens is very intricate. The black-haired dolls are dressed in white blouses with patterns. They wear black vests, and striped skirts in browns, blacks, yellows and tans. Their babushkas are painted with detailed floral patterns. Each babushka is different, yet painted either orange, green or red. Dolls #1, 4 and 7 carry bouquets of flowers. Doll #3 carries a shoulder purse. $75-90

Plate 76 Set of eight Bullet maidens. This large set of eight dolls is bullet-shaped and very detailed. They wear babushkas, blouses, vests and striped skirts. The colors vary on each doll – orange, brown, blue, green and yellow. The largest doll carries a large bouquet of white flowers. Doll #3 carries an art kit with paint brushes. Doll #4 holds books in her arms. Doll #6 carries a straw basket over her arm. $70-80

43

Plate 77 Set of nine Conical maidens. The nine dolls in this set are egg or conical-shaped. The set is 7½'' tall. The intricately painted dolls wear blouses, babushkas, vests and striped skirts. They are painted in shades of orange, blue, green and red. The largest doll carries bread and salt on a long white towel. (These are slavic symbols of hospitality.) Doll #2 carries a white dove. Dolls #3, 5 and 7 hold bouquets of orange, red or white flowers. Doll #6 has a book in her arm. $80-90

Plate 78 Six Conical maidens with baby. This 5½'' set of six is so unusual because the largest doll holds a baby wrapped in a pink bunting. The conical or egg-shaped dolls have dark brown or black hair. Their white blouses are painted with flowers. They wear black or brown vests. Each doll has a different color scheme – blue and navy blue, maroon and orange, light and dark green, and orange and red. Both the skirts and babushkas are decorated with circles and dots. The four middle dolls carry bouquets of flowers. $35-40

Plate 79 Five Conical maidens with book. The 5″ dolls in this set of five are conical or egg-shaped. The maidens have black hair and eyes. They are dressed in babushkas, blouses, vests and striped skirts. Floral designs decorate the green, red or yellow babushkas. Their white blouses are painted with floral patterns. The skirts are painted in earth tones with horizontal patterns. The largest doll holds a green book. Dolls #3 and 5 carry bouquets of flowers. $25-30

Plate 80 Five red and yellow maidens. All five dolls in this 5″ set have black hair and eyes. They are dressed alike in typical Ukrainian colors – yellow, black and red. The dolls have their hands inside red pockets. On the back of each doll is a black rectangle with geometric patterns of red and yellow. $20-25

Plate 81 Hospitality maidens. The four dolls in this 4'' set are dressed in dark blue vests, natural wood blouses and red babushkas. They have orange hair and black eyes. The largest doll carries a brown loaf of bread on a long towel (slavic symbols of hospitality). $14-20

Plate 82 Mother-of-Pearl inlaid eggs. This beautiful egg set of three is about 3'' tall. Most of the eggs have been left their natural wood tone. Vertical lines are burned into the eggs in patterns and painted black. Simple geometric shapes decorate the surface in shades of green and red. Small circles of mother-of-pearl are inlaid into the surface of the eggs. $35-40

46

MOLDAVIA

Moldavia is a Union Republic of the Soviet Union. It is located due east of Rumania and south of the Ukraine. At one time, Moldavia was an autonomous country. Like many other districts of the U.S.S.R., Moldavia produces Matreshka nesting doll sets. An unusual feature of the Moldavian sets is they appear to exclusively depict men. The author has never seen Moldavian female Matreshka sets, with the exception of the Tiraspol maidens. In contrast, most other districts produce mostly maidens. Three different male sets will be examined here.

Two male nesting sets depict St. Nick. The first set of three consists of two men and a grey rabbit. This rather serious appearing Moldavian St. Nick carries a pack full of hearts on his back signifying love. The author has been told it is a Russian custom to give Soviet children a bunny on Christmas day if they have been especially good. That is the significance of the innermost grey rabbit. Another source says St. Nick's helpers are not elves, but rather tiny hares. More likely, this set is based on nineteenth century verses by Nikolai Nekraso. The poems are about an old hunter, Grandfather Mazay. The old man rescues hordes of hares from drowning, while out hunting in the spring. He warns them to hide when summer ends or he will shoot them.

It is difficult to prove which story fits. Perhaps it is not even important. The author has wondered if the doll symbolizes holidays in a broader sense with Christmas, Easter and Valentine's Day all combined into one figure.

The second set is quite similar. This set consists of three old men figures that are identical to those described above except for size and color variations. The first set is smaller with the men wearing red jackets, green caps and green mittens. These colors often symbolize Christmas. Perhaps that is why the first set has been identified with St. Nick. In the second set, the men wear either royal blue jackets and caps or green jackets and caps with yellow mittens. This second set is more closely related to Grandfather Mazay. They all have natural wood faces, large blue eyes, pink cheeks and red mouths. They have short white beards, mustaches and fluffy white eyebrows. The men wear fur on their caps and jackets with grey clasps. All of them carry basket-like packs or pouches on their backs filled with red hearts.

The third piece is a single male figure made as a pencil box. Like traditional Matreshkas, he splits in half. His clothing depicts traditional Moldavian male garb. In other respects, he resembles the Tiraspol maidens.

These Moldavian sets are quite whimsical, well turned and painted. These sets add charm to any collection. Perhaps Moldavia will someday export female nesting dolls as well as the Tiraspol maidens to the United States.

Plate 83 Moldavia region, St. Nick or Grandfather Mazay. These two Moldavian sets of old gents are quite similar. Each man has large blue eyes, white eyebrows, mustaches, beards and hair. They wear caps, jackets, black belts, mittens and yellow woven packs filled with orange hearts on their backs. In the large 6'' set, the men wear either blue or green jackets and caps. In the small 4¼'' set, both men wear green caps and mittens and red coats. The smallest figure is a grey hare. $15-25

Plate 84 Pencil Box Man. This elegant gentleman stands 10'' tall. He is a pencil box that splits in half. The Moldavian man is dressed in typical costume for the region. He wears a tall, grey fur hat, and natural wood shirt and trousers. His clothing is decorated with orange and black triangles. He wears a yellow vest adorned with greenery and black fingerprint swirls. His orange belt completes the costume. He has black hair and facial features. $10-15

48

TIRASPOL

The village of Tiraspol lies on the eastern border of Moldavia near the Ukraine. It is located due north of the Black Sea. This southern village produces a set of Matreshka maidens that is quite different from the more traditional Moldavian sets. In fact, this set of six maidens greatly resemble the classic Semenov Matreshka maidens.

The shape of the Tiraspol doll resembles her sister Semenov and Kirov counterparts. Her face is almost identical to a Semenov maiden. The Tiraspol doll also has black "Semenov" hair and a yellow babushka. A few dolls in the set have black swirl "fingerprints" on the babushkas. The Tiraspol maiden's dress is orange. She wears a rectangular yellow apron with black swirl "fingerprints." The Semenov maidens wear rounded aprons and the bouquet becomes part of the design. These two features, the orange dress and the apron are the only visual variations from the Semenov dolls. The bouquets of the Tiraspol sets are much simpler than the Semenov flowers. The Tiraspol maidens carry large red flowers and small blue buds with greenery.

If a set of Tiraspol maiden Matreshkas is unmarked, it could easily pass for a Semenov set. The clues are very subtle. You probably would not think of Moldavia at all. Collectors should closely examine a set of Tiraspol dolls to note the differences.

Plate 85 Maidens. There are six members in this 6" set. All the maidens have black hair and eyes. They wear yellow babushkas trimmed with red flower buds and greenery. Each of their blouses and aprons are left natural wood with black fingerprint swirls. Their bouquets are made of large red flowers and small blue buds. $25-30

Plate 86 Box for Tiraspol maidens. The cardboard box for the Tiraspol maidens is silkscreened in four colors – white, brown, yellow and green.

Plate 87 Miniature Maidens. The miniature dolls in this set of three are 2½" tall. They have black hair and eyes with red mouths. The dolls are dressed in yellow babushkas and square aprons with black fingerprint swirls. Their skirts are orange, except for the baby, who is dressed in yellow. The dolls hold simple red flowers. $5-10

49

YOSCAR OLA

Yoscar Ola is a Soviet city with an Asian flavor. The city is due south of Kirov, northwest of Kazan and east of Moscow. The Matreshka dolls from this region are very small and very snugly nested. They are the most diminutive Matreshka, nested down to 1/4''.

The Marijaha dolls, as they are called, exhibit Mongul features. The oriental influence is most obvious in the facial features of the dolls. The maidens have black hair, eyes, lashes and brows. Their lips are red, while their cheeks are pink. The Marijahas wear simple dresses of either yellow or natural wood tones. The costumes are trimmed at the neckline, shoulders, cuffs and hems with black, red and green geometric bands. Sometimes orange and black embroidery is hand painted as detail. They wear red and black belts tied in front at their waists. Each doll wears a simple babushka tied and flipped under the chin. The color of the babushka is the only variation within a Marijaha set. The babushka colors used are yellow, blue and green.

Since this doll is so closely nested, even sets with many pieces inside are quite small. The sets are usually made with five or ten dolls, yet sets of 3, 4, 6, 8 and 12 are also produced. The Marijaha, reflecting the Mongul people is a lovely Matreshka and worthy of any collection.

Plate 88 Marijaha maidens. The ten dolls in this 5'' set are tightly nested together. Each doll is Oriental in appearance with black hair and eyes. They wear natural wood dresses with red belts and trim. There are three different colors of babushkas that alternate throughout the set – yellow, blue and green. The babushkas are not tied in bows, but rather are folded under their chins. $45-55

THE SOUTHERN REGIONS

The Southern regions of the Soviet Union have a definite Moslem flavor. One third of the Soviet peoples are Moslem or Oriental. In the 1100's, the Mongul Tartar warriors under the command of Ghengis Khan invaded Russia from the East. The Monguls conquered Russia and changed the vast country forever. The Asian influence can still be seen in many areas of Southern and Eastern Russia today. The Monguls intermarried with the Slavic Russians. Their descendents continue to display Mongul features. The oriental characteristics are highly visible in some of the Matreshka sets from the Southern regions, as well as those from Yoscar Ola.

The two Aiguel sets of nesting dolls are from the Southern and Eastern regions of Russia, north of the Black Sea. The oriental influence is very great, as the dolls look very Mongul-like. The two sets are very unique in that they open from the bottom and not the center as most Matreshkas do. Their hair and Oriental facial features are black. The clothing reflects their Asian ethnicity. One set consists of three males, while the other set consists of three females. The men wear jackets with long hooded headgear. The colors contrast greatly, blacks, reds, yellows and greens. Geometric swirls accent their jackets. The women wear red babushkas with lovely floral designs or caps with veils. Their dresses are lovely and are complemented with necklaces. Blacks, reds, yellows and greens are again used as primary colors to paint the Aiguel women. These two sets are beautiful, unique, expensive and rare.

The Druzba Matreshka, likewise, is made in the Southern district of the Soviet Union. She has been called "a member of the wedding party." These oriental dolls wear Moslem headbands or caps and veils. Like the Aiguel and Marijaha sets of Yoscar Ola, the Druzba sets, too, have very oriental features. The Druzba sets vary greatly in color. Their clothing is painted in simple geometric designs. Bold colors such as yellows, blues, pinks, reds, oranges, lavenders and browns are used. White dots accent their head caps or bands. The Druzba Matreshka dolls are made in sets of five. Two solid, single Druzba dolls are also manufactured. One Druzba is quite small and simple, while the other has a pointed head, detailed painting and is larger. The Druzba sets are probably the most colorful dolls of the Southern region.

Finally, the Mordva dolls are created in the Southern region. Mordva is an area southeast of Moscow. It lies south of the Volga River down to the Caspian Sea. Mordva lies west of the city of Kazan and due north of the Black Sea. The Mordva dolls have a "Turkish" influence. They do not have Oriental eyes. In fact, their eyes resemble those of the Semenov sets. Often the Mordva dolls have somber, pouting or even angry facial expressions. Five different Mordva maiden sets are included here. The dolls come in sets of 1, 3, 5 and 7. They wear the Moslem veils, caps and fringe of their native area. Some of the Mordva Matreshka dolls wear Moslem headbands. Often Mordva dolls wear round, dot beads of pink, red or green. Their clothing is usually painted in bands of color with geometric patterns throughout. The primary colors used on the Mordva dolls are red, yellow, black, green and sometimes pink. A tall, single, pencil box maiden is a rare Mordva find. The Mordva Matreshkas enjoy a special spot in many collections.

All three of these areas help to make up the Southern Region of the Soviet Union. These non-Slavic or Turkish peoples have adapted the Slavic Matreshkas and created their own version of the nested doll. They are real folk pieces and worthy of any collection.

Plate 89 Aiguel sets of males and maidens. These two sets are both unusual and beautiful. The Oriental influence is very obvious in the black facial features of these dolls. Both sets of three have unusual shapes and open at the bottom. The 3¾'' set of males is painted in black, yellow, red and dark green. Their black hair is covered by elaborate hoods with floral patterns down the back. They wear natural wood shirts and black or green jackets. The 3'' female set is painted red, yellow, black, green and natural wood. The largest doll wears a long red babushka with floral patterns of yellow and natural wood. She wears large white beads and a black dress. The two smaller maidens wear red caps and long red veils decorated with red and yellow ball fringe. Their coats are painted green, red and natural wood tones. The maidens have black hair. Rare $30-50

Plate 90 Druzba maidens front view. The five dolls in the 5″ set are very Oriental in appearance. Each doll has black hair covered by a cap of green, purple, brown, orange or blue. Over the cap is a veil, each also a different color. They wear clothes with geometric patterns in shades of brown, orange, blue, red, violet, green and pink. $35-45

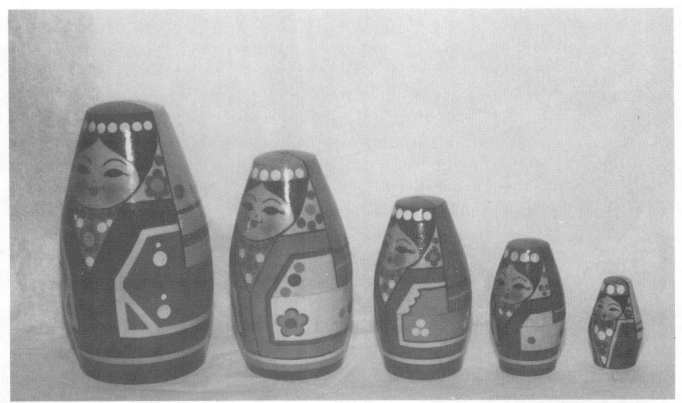

Plate 91 Druzba maidens side view. The five veils and head pieces are more visible on this 5″ set. Each doll is painted with a different color scheme. The veils are yellow, green, orange, brown and natural wood. Each veil has two bands of color at the bottom in various combinations – red, green and yellow. $35-45

Plate 92 Druzba three solid maidens. All three dolls are solid pieces in unusual shapes. They are 2-2¼'' tall. All three dolls have black hair and eyes. The smallest doll has a painted face with a yellow babushka, blouse and apron. Two red apples are painted on the apron. Her skirt is painted dark blue. The two larger dolls are fat and pointed on the top. Their clothing is very detailed and painted primarily in red and orange. They wear black plaid skirts and have floral patterns painted on the back of their babushkas. $3-10

Plate 93 Mordva set of seven maidens. The seven black-haired maidens in this 6½'' set have very somber expressions. They wear red babushkas with yellow bands around their heads. The dolls are dressed in natural wood dresses and multi-striped aprons. The stripes are painted yellow, pink and green with black geometric designs over the colors. $35-45

53

Plate 94 Mordva set of five maidens. This 4½'' set of five dolls has a most unusual shape. The black-haired dolls have large pink cheeks. They wear yellow caps trimmed with red ball fringe. Over the caps they wear long, red veils with black fringe. The dolls have no arms in their natural wood dresses. Their rectangle aprons are painted in horizontal stripes of red, green and yellow. The top stripe is decorated with five green circles. Rare $26-40

Plate 95 Mordva maidens. (Left) The five maidens in this flat-topped set stand 4¼'' tall. The maidens have very stern expressions. Each doll has black hair and red dot cheeks. They wear armless natural wood dresses with rectangle aprons. The aprons are painted with horizontal bands of red, yellow and green. Each doll wears a red babushka and a yellow band around her head. The largest doll wears a red dot necklace. (Right) The three maidens in this set stand 4½'' tall. The armless dolls are painted with various bands of color – black, red, yellow and pink. Round circles of pink and green decorate the dresses. Each doll wears a red veil over her black hair. $15-30

Plate 96 Mordva maiden box. This tall, thin, single box is 7¼'' tall. She has black hair and eyes. Her clothing is decorated with horizontal stripes of red, black, green, yellow and pink. Both her headdress and dot beads are painted red. $15-25

In the U.S.S.R. today, virtually every region has designed, developed and produced its own Matreshka doll sets. Yet very little published information has been available regarding regional variations in design and style. Therefore, the task of identifying the specific provenance of dolls from the Soviet Union can be both difficult and perplexing.

Sometimes Soviet Matreshkas are imported by individuals or importers without identification. Some sets are brought to the U.S. by new immigrants. Most Matreshka dolls are marked only with, "Made in U.S.S.R." The collector then has no data to identify the regional origin of the set. That does not imply the sets are not valuable, desirable or collectible. It merely means currently, the region of origin is unknown. In fact, it is quite a thrill to be able to identify a set after it has been an "unknown" for awhile.

Twenty-one sets are included here in this section because their exact origins within the Soviet Union are not available. However, all twenty-one sets were definitely made within the Soviet borders. The designs and style prevent them from being included from the principle regions of Semenov, Zagorsk, Kirov, Brest, Polkhov Maidan and the Ukraine. One problem contributing to the difficulty occurs when a region varies the style through the years.

Two single types of Matreshkas are crafted like the sets, but they stand alone. One type is a hollow doll or box. The second type is a solid figure, like the smallest doll in a Matreshka set. A male box is made in regions unknown. Mr. Mushroom is a traditional Russian folk figure. You remove his mushroom cap to reveal a hollow interior. He is possibly from the Brest region.

Penguins are a recurring theme for Russian Matreshka nesting dolls (and other countries). The set from the Brest region includes four white and blue penguins. Two other sets of penguins included here are unidentifiable. Since they do not wear costumes, it is most difficult to pinpoint a region. The two sets could be from the Moscow region. Both sets are small. One set is composed of a mother with two children inside. The other set of two is a mother and her baby. The penguin sets are painted true to nature, black and white.

Very few Russian nesting sets mix male figures with female dolls. The Semenov Good Family Man and early Zagorsk sets included boys with maiden sets. There is such a set of four Matreshka dolls from regions unknown. The three largest dolls are mustached men. The smallest doll is a little girl dressed in a simple orange dress with long black braids. Most likely, this set was made in the Southern region. The dolls look Turkic or Oriental. The men wear muted dark clothing in hues of blue, green, red, orange and yellow. They have black eyes, black hair and unusual red noses. This set is probably one of the most unusual Russian sets the author has ever seen.

Another rare find from regions unknown is a matte-finish Father Frost (Russian Santa Claus). He is the only Matreshka doll the author has seen that has no gloss at all. He wears a red coat and cap trimmed with fur and decorated with white snowflakes. His long, white beard covers up most of his pink face. He has tiny black eyes and red cheeks with a red nose. Inside Father Frost are solid figures similar to the Semenov counting sets. The inside contents vary from set to set. A round, red package tied with a white bow is usually included. Sometimes the head of a man is a part of the set. The purpose of this piece is a mystery. Usually two or three maidens are included. The maidens are very simple with natural wood bodies, black hair and black dot eyes. They wear blue or red babushkas. The set was purchased by the author in the early 1970's. Another collector located the set in Belgium in 1981.

Three maiden sets of elongated, muted color Matreshka dolls could be from the Zagorsk region. These sets are from old collections and stylistic changes do occur over the years. The maidens are fully painted including their faces. They are one of the few maiden sets that do not hold a bouquet of garden flowers, also characteristic of Zagorsk. The author doubts if these sets are manufactured anymore.

Two tiny sets of three maidens, one with "carrot colored" hair and the other with brown hair are very similar. These tiny sets could be from Zagorsk or Kirov, or places unknown. The tiny sets are left a natural wood tone with black accents. The largest dolls in the two sets hold blue and red dot flowers. Their basic design strongly suggests Kirov, yet Kirov dolls are never brown haired. Zagorsk sets are always totally painted. Therefore, these sets remain mysteries.

Two other maiden sets of three are produced from unknown regions, with only minor variations. These maidens resemble Semenov sets but have unique differences. The eyes and lips are not typical of Semenov sets. The maidens hold large poppies and sprays of wheat. They were probably made in a region close to Semenov, but for now they are unidentified.

A set of seven maidens is unique for several reasons. The Matreshka dolls have alternating hair color – blonde, brown, blonde, brown and three black haired dolls. The author has never seen hair treated in this manner before. This set has also been painted with very unusual colors – salmon pink, wine purple, navy blue and grass green. The largest doll has long eyelashes and a large open smile. She is quite beautiful.

The last six maiden sets are all different, but the author strongly feels they were made in the same region. The smallest set of four is quite a miniature and simple in design. The primary decorations on the doll are composed of "dots." The dolls have polka dots on their babushkas and flowers on their poneveras made from dots. Even their eyes and mouths are designated by "dots." This brown-haired set is extremely simple.

The second set of four dolls is larger in size. She, too, wears a babushka decorated with flowers made from dots in different colors. Her apron, likewise is decorated with "dot" flowers and greenery. The black haired Matreshkas wear green and orange throughout the set. Half the dolls wear green babushkas and aprons with orange dresses, while the other half wear orange babushkas and aprons with green dresses.

The five Matreshkas in the third set are blonde. The dresses and babushkas are left the natural wood tone. These dolls, too, have "dots" for eyes, mouths and buttons down the front of their dresses. The natural tone babushkas are decorated with "dot" flowers on bands of color at the hemline. These bands match the buttons of other dolls in the set. Red, green, orange, pale blue and yellow are used in a pleasant manner.

Finally, the last three sets of seven and ten dolls are quite similar to each other with minor color variations. These sets are more detailed versions of the "second dot set" with lighter hair.

Some old sets are difficult to distinguish because they are one-of-a-kinds, often worn, in poor condition and scarce. The set included here has lost several members over the years. The black haired maiden wears a babushka, blue vest and striped skirt. One smaller inside doll is her son. He wears a blue jacket. She resembles some Polish sets.

The final set is most unique and possibly a one-of-a-kind. It is a set of four black men. The owner believes it is a Russian set because of the wood used, the lathe style and shape, as well as the painting techniques. However, the subject matter is most unusual as a Russian theme. Unfortunately, the set is not marked in any way. The four black men are identical except for size. They wear white shirts, blue jackets and red string ties. Their coal black skin barely shows two black eyes, red lips and white teeth. This is indeed a most unusual set!

Every set of Russian Matreshka dolls has its own unique expression, style and personality. Even if the origins of sets are not known, they still have strong appeal. Collectors appreciate every single set, even those with pasts cloaked in mystery.

Plate 97 Mr. Mushroom box. Mr. Mushroom stands 4¾" tall and his mushroom cap is removeable. Inside you store small items. Most of his body is made up of his natural wood face. He has large blue eyes, grey hair and a long grey beard. His large mushroom cap is maroon with white polka dots. He wears a natural wood shirt trimmed in red and a plain brown vest. $8-15

Plate 98 Penguins. Both sets of penguins have black heads, wings and backs. Their breasts are painted white. The birds in the large 4¾" set of two have red beaks and feet. The birds in the smaller 3½" set of three have orange beaks and feet. The two small penguins in this set are solid and nest as twins inside the mother. $7-10

Plate 99 Three men with little girl. This 8″ set of four is very unusual. The smallest doll is a little girl within a set of men. All four dolls have black hair and eyes. The men are dressed in shirts, trousers and belts of blue, green and orange in different combinations. The girl has long braids and wears an orange dress. $15-25

Plate 100 Father Frost with girls. Father Frost is 4¾″ in this matte-finish set. He has a pink face, red nose and black eyes. His coat and cap are decorated with white snowflakes and white fur trim. His long, white beard covers most of his stomach. Inside Father Frost nests a red round package and solid little girls. The girls are wearing natural wood dresses and either red or turquoise babushkas. Rare $20-30

Plate 101 Elongated maidens I. This 4¾'' set of four is tall and old. The maidens have painted faces and black hair. Each doll wears a different color babushka, blouse, vest and skirt. The muted colors used are white, yellow, brown, green, red and blue. $25-35

Plate 102 Elongated maidens II. The four blonde maidens in this old set of four stand 4¾'' tall. They are dressed in babushkas, blouses, vests and skirts of different muted colors – white, red, tan, blue, yellow and green. $25-35

Plate 103 Elongated maidens III. Each brown haired maiden in this set of four wears a different color combination. The 4¾'' set is tall, old and elongated. The dolls wear babushkas, blouses, vests and skirts in different muted colors – white, pink, tan, red, green, blue and yellow.
$25-35

Plate 104 Tiny maidens. These two tiny sets are 1¾''-2'' tall. Most of the dolls are unpainted natural wood. They have either brown or orange hair. Most of the detail is rendered with black ink. They wear rounded aprons with bouquets of red and blue dot flowers.
$12-15

60

Plate 105 Poppy maidens with wheat. Both sets of maidens are 3¾'' tall. Each set contains three maidens with black hair, eyes and long eyelashes. They wear natural wood blouses and aprons and red skirts. Their babushkas are yellow with black fingerprint swirls. Large orange or pink poppies and shafts of wheat make up their bouquets. $14-18

Plate 106 Multi-colored hair maidens. This lovely set of seven dolls stand 5¼'' tall. They have very happy expressions. Dolls #1 and 3 are blonde. Dolls #2 and 4 have brown hair while the three smallest dolls are black-haired. The dolls wear natural wood aprons with bouquets of pink, yellow and blue flowers. They wear babushkas and dresses of unusual, assorted colors – bright red, lemon yellow, grass green, salmon pink, wine purple and dark blue. $30-40

Plate 107 Simple dot maidens. This simple set of four stands about 2½'' tall. The dolls have brown hair with dot noses and mouths. Their babushkas and jumpers are painted in alternating colors of pink, green and pale blue. Simple dot flowers grace the front of the jumpers. Each babushka is decorated with white polka dots. $10-15

Plate 108 Set of four dot maidens. Each black-haired doll in this 4'' set wears a babushka, natural wood dress and apron. The four dolls are painted in alternating colors of green, red and orange. Their aprons and babushkas are painted with dot flowers and polka dots in shades of orange, white, blue and yellow. $15-20

Plate 109 Blonde dot maidens. The five blonde maidens in this 5'' set are dressed in natural wood dresses and babushkas. The babushkas are trimmed in bands of different colors and then decorated with white dot flowers. The bands match the dot buttons down the front of the dress in shades of red, pale blue, pale green, orange and yellow. The babushkas are also painted with large, red strawberries and greenery. $8-18

Plate 110 Set of seven dot maidens. This 5'' set of seven is also decorated with dots. The blonde maidens wear babushkas, blouses, aprons and skirts in assorted colors – olive green, yellow, orange, white, blue and red. The babushkas are painted with lovely dot flowers. $40-45

Plate 111 Set of ten dot maidens I. The 10 maidens in this 6'' set have light brown hair. They are dressed in babushkas, blouses, skirts and jumpers in an alternating color pattern. The babushkas and aprons are decorated with white and orange dot flowers. The clothing colors are green, turquoise, blue, orange, red and yellow. $45-55

Plate 112 Set of 10 dot maidens II. This 6'' set of 10 are decorated with dots and dot flowers. All the blonde maidens wear babushkas, blouses, jumpers and aprons. The babushkas and aprons are painted with white orange dot flowers. The colors used on the clothing are red, orange, green, lime green and yellow. $45-55

Plate 113 Antique maiden & son. There are many missing members from this old 4¾'' set. The black-haired mother is garbed in a babushka, white blouse, blue vest and red and blue stripped shirt. Her small son is black haired with a white shirt and blue trousers. Rare $15-25

Plate 114 Black men. This set of 4 is so unusual because of its subject matter. The dolls are exactly alike, except for size. The black men have smiling red mouths and black eyes. They wear white shirts, light blue jackets and red string ties. Rare. $25-35

64

POLAND

Poland is a country rich in folk art and folklore. She was greatly influenced by her vast neighbor to the east, the U.S.S.R. In fact, from 1795 to 1918, Poland did not exist as a sovereign state. Her lands were divided among Russia, Germany and Austria. Like the Russians, the Poles are Slavic people with similar traditions and folklore. Nesting dolls, which developed in Poland after first being made in Russia, have enjoyed a sound place in the folk art of the country.

Anne Pellowski, in her book, *The Story Vine*, presents two reasons why Matreshka* dolls were developed and survived in Slavic Poland. The grandmother figure is quite common and very predominant in the folktales of Poland. The nesting dolls symbolize several generations, the oldest and largest often being Grandmother or Baba. The Poles easily absorbed the nesting dolls into their culture, because of the folklore. A second influence which has survived to the present is the prevalence of the Marzanna customs in rural Poland. The Marzanna is a straw or wooden figure depicting the ancient pagan goddess of Death. In late winter, the Poles carry the Marzanna out of the village and destroy it. The old woman goddess is either burned or drowned. Pellowski states that a doll is sometimes hidden inside the Marzanna effigy and taken out before the goddess figure is destroyed. This symbol of life out of death represents the coming of spring. The Marzanna festivals are unique to the peasants of Slavic countries.

Today, Poland's cottage industries are keeping alive the rich folk art of their country. While the communist government of Poland controls the marketing of the folk arts and crafts, many objects are still created at the local level. Even today, one of Poland's most famous products is the whimsical nesting doll. As a group, they function primarily as children's toys rather than objects of art. In contrast, the Russian Matreshka nesting dolls are much more delicate, detailed and artistic. As a result, the Soviet dolls are more valued by adult collectors. However, you cannot find a more appealing, solid, and fun toy than a Polish nesting set.

Polish nesting dolls are lathe made of various pine woods. They are spray painted in large, flat areas of color in an overlapping style. Smaller details are hand-painted. Unique to many Polish sets are the protruding noses pegged onto the largest doll in the set. The dolls are spray varnished and, in assembly line fashion, are nested to sell.

Unlike Russian Matreshkas, the Polish sets are quite similar to each other in design, expression and workmanship. They lack the varied, noticeable, regional differences of their Russian counterparts. In fact, there are only three known basic Polish types. The first type encompasses most of the Polish sets made today. The most identifying feature of this first type is the protruding nose on the largest doll of the set. All the fairy tale sets, eggs and families included here belong to this group.

The second type of Polish Matreshkas are produced in the town of Zakopane on the Czech border. These dolls are quite small and delicate. Zakopane maiden dolls are blue eyed with black hair. They wear black blouses and suits with vertical stripes. The suits include jackets and skirts in several colors. One set of six maidens is made with three different color variations. The Zakopane Matreshka dolls are a fairly recent import to the United States.

The third type of Polish Matreshka dolls are from the town of Nowysacz. Nowysacz lies in the province of Cracow, near Zakopane, on the Czech border. In contrast, this third type of Polish Matreshka dolls are large and rotund. They are very simple in shape, almost egg like. These maidens wear traditional babushkas and varied peasant costumes. The hair color ranges from bright blonde to warm browns and coal blacks. They have eyes of blue, brown and black. The most identifying feature of these sets of four, five, six and seven dolls are their large, round, red cheeks.

Many maiden Polish sets are manufactured. The Polish nesting dolls are most commonly grouped in sets of three. Maiden sets of four, five, six and seven sets exist as well. The largest known sets contain seven dolls, which is a small number in comparison to their Russian counterparts. Most maiden sets consist of women wearing babushkas or kerchiefs. One unique set contains bareheaded ladies with bun hairstyles. Another unique set represents Dutch girls and their hats reflect the winged caps of Holland. In a few sets, the women wear the tall or rounded caps of their provinces. Most of these ladies split in half to hold their smaller sisters. There are a few rare sets that open at the bottom. Two examples of these are Cinderella and Snow White. One unusual set of three shares a common base.

A number of Polish sets are based on fairy tales made famous by the Brothers Grimm. The fairy tale sets produced include Cinderella, the three little pigs, Hansel and Gretal with a gingerbread house, Little Red Riding Hood, Aladdin and his magic lamp, Rumpelstiltskin, Snow White and the Seven Dwarfs, the Nutcracker Suite and Chicken Little. Cinderella, Snow White and Aladdin are difficult to locate now. They are a real prize when discovered by a collector!

Unlike Russian sets, Poland creates several family sets. Three older examples of families each contain four members. One of these portrays a set of snowpeople, another depicts a family nested inside a man in a grey coat. A third set of four is a Dutch family. More recently produced families are, in contrast, made in groups of three. Most often, the families consist of a father, mother and son. On occasion, the family group includes a mother, daughter and son. There are also two different sailor families produced. Finally, three types of peasant families are manufactured. One set is dressed in white and pale yellow. Another wears navy blue and red. The third is a musician family with

*Russian spelling, Matryoshka; Polish spelling, Matroszka.

the father dressed in red and holding a brown violin. This set is sometimes known as the "man from Kielce." Each family is different and reflects its own personality.

Sets that contain only male figures appear to be much more common in Poland than in Russia. For example, Poland produces a set of soldiers dressed in red and white. One particularly odd theme selected by Polish craftsmen is the American Plains Indian. He is also known as the "Mountaineer." "The Country Squire" or "The Man In Orange" is a particularly nice set. It has also been called "the butcher, the baker and the candlestick maker." A similar set, sometimes called the Baron, depicts a man with a bright sash around his waist and contains a bottle of wine and a mug. These male dolls parallel the maidens in dimensions and uniformity.

A variety of Polish nesting egg sets are manufactured. Sets of three, four, five and six are known to exist. Some eggs are hand painted while others are wood-burned. Five types of egg sets contain animals. The lathe-turned animals are rabbits, chicks, ducks, lambs and owls. The chicks are based on the fairy tale, "Chicken Little." One very pretty egg holds a young girl. As mentioned earlier, both the Nutcracker Suite and Rumpelstiltskin are egg bowling sets. Egg sets are often included in nesting doll collections.

Poland manufactures nesting pears and apple sets. At least three different Polish cider sets have been produced through the years. The cider sets consist of a large apple with small wooden dishes inside. Occasionally the cider sets include a table. These nesting fruits are not dolls but are also often included in nesting doll collections.

Polish artists have created some charming bowling sets. These sets usually include two small wooden balls. Most of these sets contain nine pins, although sets of seven and four are also produced. The figures containing these sets vary greatly in form. One egg-shaped set contains soldiers as pins. Two varieties of this "Nutcracker Suite" are known, one painted in red and the other in blue. The head pin soldier is identified by a red tossle on the top of his helmet. A second egg-shaped set is known as "Rumpelstiltskin." The egg itself is painted midnight blue with the moon and stars above. Two figures of Rumpelstiltskin appear on the egg. The nine pins are represented as elves, all similar with only color variations.

Another type of bowling set comes in human form. Snow White contains seven pins, depicting her friends the dwarfs. The keen observer will note that these pins are an earlier form of the Rumpelstiltskin elves mentioned above. Snow White is painted in shades of blue. She cradles the fateful apple in her hands.

Mushroom shaped houses represent still another distinct type of bowling set. Two variations exist, distinguished primarily by size. The larger has a chimney, a red roof with white polka dots, windows and is circled by flowers. Inside dwell nine pins, identical to Rumpelstiltskin's dwarfs The small mushroom house is more simple in design. Decoration includes a red polka dot roof and green grass around a white base. Only four dwarfs reside here.

Finally, Polish craftsmen have created a large white bowling pin. The pin is decorated with red dot flowers. Inside are two red, wooden balls and nine, natural wood pins.

One rare Polish nesting set portrays a rocket ship. Although quite primitive in execution, it reflects our modern world's fascination with space travel. The ship is painted blue, red, yellow and white. Three cosmonauts dressed in grey space suits with blue oxygen tanks on their backs nest inside. This set was produced in the early 1970's.

In the early 1970's Polish nesting dolls were inexpensive and readily available here in the United States. Since the early 1980's, the political climate between the U.S. and Poland has deteriorated. As a result, official trade between the two countries has virtually ceased. Polish nesting dolls, once so common, are now difficult to locate. Most sets are now imported through Canada. New designs are unavailable and some of the older sets are no longer being produced. Some Polish craftsmen report they have neither wood nor paint in abundance. This lack of materials also curtails creation of inexpensive sets. Polish wood is reserved for more artistic carvings and religious figures. Hopefully, in the not too distant figure, the flow of these delightful examples of folk art will resume and the supply of Polish nested dolls will once again be plentiful in America.

Plate 115 Maidens that open at the bottom. (Left) This cheerful set of three dolls is 5" tall. The mother has blue eyes, a protruding nose and brown hair. She wears a white babushka, blouse and apron. Her long jumper is bright red. She holds two yellow flowers in her hands. The two little girls are blonde. The larger girl wears a black and brown cape, green skirt and white apron. The small girl wears a red cape and green skirt. (Right) This 6" set of three dolls is unusual for two reasons. The largest doll opens at the bottom and not in the middle. The smallest doll is a boy which is odd in a set of maidens. The mother has flesh tone skin, a protruding nose and black hair. She wears a green skirt, red apron, orange shawl and white babushka. The daughter is also black haired. She wears a white babushka and skirt, red vest, pale blue apron and large bow at her neckline. The son wears a black hat and trousers and red shirt. $12-20

Plate 116 Maiden sets of six and three. (Left) This set of six dolls is wide and tall – 6¾''. These typical Polish maidens wear babushkas of either green or red. The dolls' clothing colors alternate in patterns. The largest and third dolls wear yellow. The second and fourth dolls wear pale green with white aprons. The fifth doll has yarn braids and is dressed in black, white and pale blue. The baby is dressed in white and has a tuft of yellow yarn hair. (Right) In this set of 5'' maidens, all three wear striped dresses of white, yellow and green. The largest doll has a red babushka, the middle doll has a green one, while the little girl is bareheaded.$15-35

Plate 117 Dutch maidens. This large set of six represents Dutch girls in regional costumes. All but the baby have brown hair; she is a blonde. In this 7'' set, the maidens wear either Dutch capes or babushkas of white, blue or yellow. They wear skirts, aprons, blouses and vests in assorted colors - red, yellow, blue, white, black and turquoise. Photo - courtesy of The Children's Museum of Indianapolis. $25-35

Plate 118 Maidens with bun hairstyles. The three maidens in this set are tall and thin. In the 5'' set, all the maidens wear a hairstyle with a bun on the back of their heads. Their clothing consists of black blouses and either red or green skirts, with accents in assorted colors. Photo - courtesy of The Children's Museum of Indianapolis. $15-20

Plate 119 Small set of three maidens. The three girls in this small set can be found in the larger sets as the three smallest members. The largest girl is 2½'' tall. She has blue eyes and brown hair. Her babushka is red and her blouse and apron are white. She wears a striped cape and skirt in green tones. The middle girl has yellow yarn braids. Her clothing is painted black, and pale blue with a white apron. The baby is garbed in white with a tuft of blonde yarn hair. $5-10

Plate 120 Tiny set of three girls. The three girls in this set are short and fat. They are 2'' tall with dark brown hair and simple dress. The largest doll wears a red babushka and yellow dress with green and red stripes. The middle girl has a green babushka and turquoise dress. The baby is dressed in white. $5-10

Plate 121 Zakopane maidens, red and natural. Both of these 3½'' sets of maidens are alike except they have clothing color differences. All the maidens from the Zakopane region have black hair. These sets of six have blue eyes. The dolls on the left wear red dresses and green babushkas. The dolls on the right are dressed in natural wood dresses with multi-colored stripes. Their babushkas are red. $16-25

Plate 122 Zakopane maidens, multicolored. This 3½'' set of six is another color variation. The blue eyed, black haired dolls are dressed in three styles. They wear orange babushkas and green dresses, or red babushkas with natural wood dresses, or green babushkas with red dresses. $16-25

Plate 123 Zakopane maidens, red (opens at bottom) and orange. (Left) This 2¼'' set of three is most unusual because they share a common base. The bottom of the largest doll comes off to hold the two smaller dolls inside. The black haired, blue eyed maidens have green babushkas, black blouses and red skirts and capes. (Right) All four of the maidens in this 2¾'' split at the skirt line. They have blue eyes and black hair. Their babushkas are green and their black blouses are accented with red. Their orange capes and skirts have multicolored stripes. $9-15

Plate 124 Zakopane maidens, red (3) and green (4). (Left) This tiny set of three is only 1¾'' tall and very slender. The black haired, blue-eyed beauties have pink dot hands. Their babushkas are green and their black blouses are laced with yellow. They wear red capes and skirts with black stripes. (Right) This 2¾'' set of four dolls is another color variation. The blue eyes, black haired maidens wear red babushkas. White ruffles accent their black blouses. Their skirts and capes are green with vertical stripes of other colors. $9-15

Plate 125 Zakopane maidens (6). These somber black eyed, black haired maidens alternate colors in their dress. The sets of six stands 2½'' tall. All the dolls have black blouses. Red and medium blue are the colors of the babushkas and the skirts and capes. $10-15

Plate 126 Nowysacz maidens (black hair) in green babushka (6). In this set of 5'' dolls, all six are dressed alike. The black haired maidens have large red cheeks. They wear green babushkas and skirts. The white blouses are accented by green bead necklaces. The plain pink vests are closed with a shell decoration. $14-20

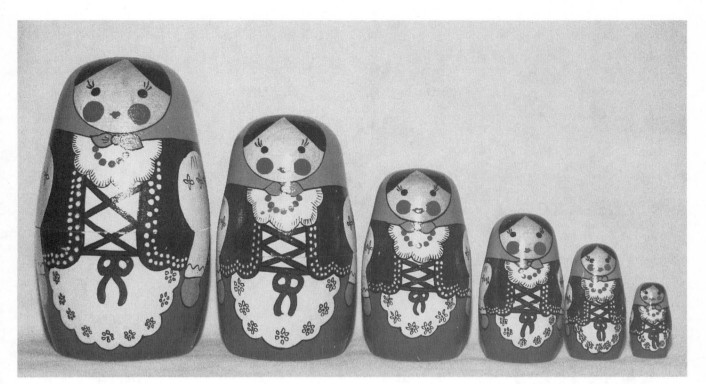

Plate 127 Nowysacz maidens (black hair) in pink babushka (6). These six black-haired beauties have dark eyelashes and red cheeks. The 5'' set is made with matching dolls. All six wear pink babushkas, dark green vests with white dot accents, white blouses and aprons, red bead necklaces and skirts. $14-20

Plate 128 Nowysacz maidens (black hair) in turquoise babushka (6). This 5'' doll set contains six dolls. All six maidens wear turquoise babushkas and bead necklaces. The blouses and aprons are wavy and white. They wear red laced vests with blue flowers and pink skirts. $14-20

Plate 129 Nowysacz maidens (black hair) in red babushka (5). There are five dolls in this 4″ set. These black hair dolls wear red babushkas and red skirts. Their coats are solid green with red flowers at the hem. No arms show. Only a bit of white apron appears beneath the coat. $12-18

Plate 130 Nowysacz miadens (brown hair) in red babushka (5). This 4″ set of 5 dolls is simple in shape. It is the only Nowysacz set that has brown haired maidens. The dolls wear red babushkas and red skirts. They wear solid green coats with red flowers at the hemline. A small bit of white apron shows beneath the coat. Their arms do not show. $12-18

Plate 131 Nowysacz maidens (black hair) in green babushka. In this lovely set of five, the dolls have full eyes and lashes. The set is 4″ tall with matching dolls. Each black haired doll wears a green babushka, yellow vest, red skirt, white blouse and apron. The apron has elaborate fringe around the border. The dolls carry bouquets of red, blue and white flowers. (5) $12-18

Plate 132 Nowysacz maidens (black hair) in blue babushka (5). This 4″ set of five dolls is dressed in blues. Each doll wears a blue babushka and matching skirt. Their laced vests are a darker blue. The white blouses and aprons match with eyelet patterns. $12-18

Plate 133 Nowysacz maidens (black hair) in pale blue babushka (5). The five dolls in this 4'' set have black hair with wispy bangs. The dolls wear pale blue babushkas decorated with blue flowers. They wear dark blue vests with red laces, red skirts, white blouses and round white aprons. $12-18

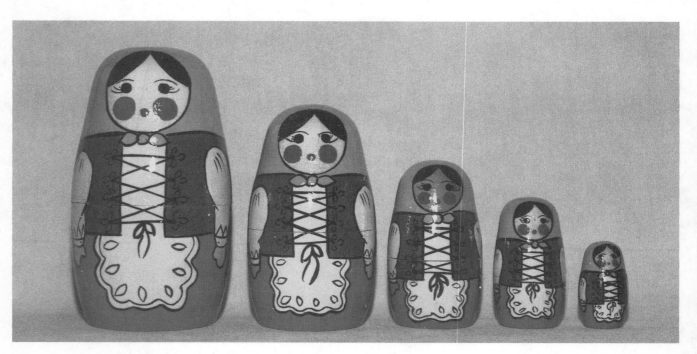

Plate 134 Nowysacz maidens (black hair) in yellow babushka (5). All five dolls in this 4'' set have large red cheeks. Their black hair is covered by yellow babushkas. The dolls wear white blouses and aprons. Their green vests are laced in black. The salmon pink skirts are a very nice touch. $12-18

Plate 135 Nowysacz maidens (black hair) in pink babushka (5). The black haired dolls in this 4″ set of 5 are all dressed alike. They wear pink babushkas with green and white flower patterns. Each doll wears a white blouse and dark green vest buttoned in front. Their skirts are red. The red bead necklaces match the skirts and the red cherries on the bottom of the white aprons. $12-18

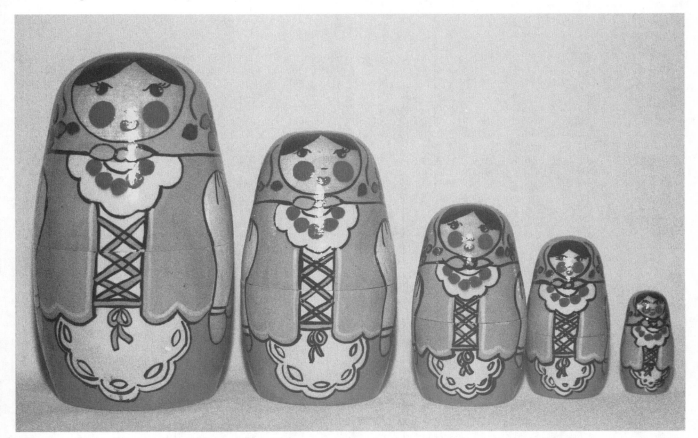

Plate 136 Nowysacz maidens (black hair) in turquoise babushka (5). Soft shades make this 4″ set of 5 dolls so pretty. All 5 wear turquoise laced vests and babushkas. Yellow flowers border the hem of the scarf. The maidens wear white blouses and aprons with pink skirts. A string of red beads completes their look. $12-18

76

Plate 137 Nowysacz maidens (black hair) in azure babushka (5). All five dolls in this 4″ set are dressed alike. Each black-haired doll wears an azure blue babushka with dark blue flowers. The flowers are the same shade as the vests. The vests are closed by a single white button. They wear white blouses and aprons and red skirts. Four pink tassles are painted on the front of the vests. A single strand of pink beads matches the pink dots on the sleeves of the dresses. $12-18

Plate 138 Nowysacz maidens (blonde) in red and green (4). These four red cheeked maidens are very somber blondes. The set stands 3¼″ tall. All four wear green babushkas and skirts. Their long vests are red with vertical green stripes. White blouses and aprons are barely visible. $10-15

Plate 139 Nowysacz maidens (blonde) in red, white and blue (4). This maiden set of four stands 3¼'' tall. She has a very somber expression on her natural wood face. Her blonde hair is covered by a plain red babushka. She wears a navy blue and red vest, white blouse and apron and red skirt. $10-15

Plate 140 Nowysacz maidens (black hair) in white babushka (4). Four maidens nest in this 3¼'' set. The maidens wear white babushkas with tiny red flowers decorating the surface. Their aprons and blouses are also white. Navy blue jackets with red trim and red skirts complete their clothing. The black haired dolls hold their natural wood hands at their waist. $10-15

Plate 141 Nowysacz maidens in white cap and green babushka (4). This 3¼'' set of four maidens is most unusual because no hair is exposed. The maidens wear white caps with green babushkas over them. Each doll wears a white blouse and apron. Their black vests are laced with yellow ties. Red skirts complete their clothing. $10-15

Plate 142 Nowysacz maidens (orange hair) in striped vest (4). This set of four maidens is unique for Poland because the dolls have orange hair. All the dolls in the 3¼'' set wear red babushkas, white blouses, red skirts and blue vests. Their aprons are painted with multi-color stripes. $10-15

Plate 143 Fairy tale sets. Four favorite fairy tales are represented here. (Left) The set of three little pigs stands 6'' tall. Each pink pig wears a scarf and hat in shades of yellow, green, blue, white and red. (Midleft) The 5'' set is Little Red Riding Hood, Grandma and the big bad wolf. The grey wolf wears a red hat and vest. His large necktie is blue. White-haired Grandma, in red and yellow, wears her glasses. Little Red wears a red cape and cap and a white polka dot dress. She carries a yellow basket in her hands. (Mid-right) Lovely Cinderella, her fairy godmother and white bird is a 7'' set. The fairy is dressed in shades of turquoise. She holds her magic wand and a glass slipper in her hands. Cinderella is wearing a lovely white gown with red ribbons. Inside Cinderella nests the small white bird. (Right) Hansel and Gretel are nested with the witch inside the 6'' Gingerbread house. The yellow house has a brown roof and red chimney. It is decorated with white and yellow candies. The white-haired witch is wearing a red babushka, pink skirt, green plaid cape and holds a yellow broom in her hands. Gretel is dressed in yellow, while Hansel wears a yellow hat, white shirt and short blue trousers. Cinderella is rare. $13-25

Plate 144 Aladdin, the Genie and magic lamp. Another favorite tale is seen in this 5'' set of three. Aladdin and the genie wear yellow and red striped turbans on their heads. They sit with their arms crossed with red trousers and black shoes. The genie has a white beard and wears a turquoise shirt. Aladdin is garbed in a green shirt. He grows a black beard and mustache. The small lamp is painted turquoise and white. Photo - courtesy of The Children's Museum of Indianapolis. Rare $20-25

Plate 145 Rumpelstiltskin (front view). The egg in this set of 12 is 4'' tall. This bowling set consists of nine dwarfs with white beards. They are dressed in caps, shirts and pants of various colors – red, orange, green, turquoise, blue and yellow. Two wooden red balls are included in the game. The egg is painted a dark night blue. A red and yellow crescent moon and stars hang in the sky. Rumpelstiltskin is painted on the egg with a long white beard. He is dressed in red and yellow. A large green and yellow evergreen grows behind him. $15-20

Plate 146 Rumpelstiltskin (rear view). On the rear of this egg, Rumpelstiltskin faces right. Behind him is a fire of yellow and red. He holds a lantern of red and yellow as he stands firmly on the ground. $15-20

Plate 147 Snow White and the Seven Dwarfs. 7'' Snow White is a lovely holder for this 10 piece bowling set. Snow White wears a dress and long cape in shades of white and turquoise. A yellow crown graces her head. Inside, seven white-bearded dwarfs nest with two red wooden balls. The dwarfs wear caps, shirts and pants in assorted colors – red, orange, green, turquoise and yellow. Rare. Photo - courtesy of The Children's Museum of Indianapolis. $25-35

Plate 148 The Nutcracker Suite. Nine soldiers and two red wooden balls fit inside this 4'' egg. Named for the famous ballet, this bowling set contains soldiers dressed in black helmets, white trousers and blue and yellow jackets. The kingpin has a yellow top to his helmet. The egg is painted with soldiers all around the surface. They are costumed in the same uniform as the soldiers inside. $15-20

Plate 149 Chicken Little, rabbits and ducks. These three egg sets contain four animals each. (Left) The 4'' rabbit egg is painted pale blue with a brown bunny. Inside are four red rabbits. (Middle) The duck egg is 5½'' tall. The egg is painted a dark blue with rows of adult yellow ducks and red ducklings. Inside nest four yellow ducks with red beaks. (Right) The Chicken Little egg is 4'' tall. The egg is painted with running chicks, reflecting the story of Chicken Little and the falling sky. The egg is white and pale blue with yellow chicks. The four chicks are yellow with red beaks and feet. $14-20

Plate 150 Snow family. Frosty and his family of four is about 5'' tall. All four snow people are painted white. Frosty wears a black top hat, green scarf and green mittens. His red nose sticks out like a carrot. He has protruding white cheeks as well. Mrs. Frosty wears a red bonnet and green mittens. The daughter wears a green cap and mittens. The baby has no clothing at all. Rare. $25-35

83

Plate 151 Grey family (old version). Each member of this 4½'' family is dressed in folk clothing. The father has large black eyes and a brown mustache. His grey coat is accented in red. His flat hat is bright yellow. Mother wears a tall black hat, red blouse and striped skirt. The girl is lovely in her red and black clothing. The tiny infant is dressed in white.
$15-20

Plate 152 Grey family (new version). All four members of this 5½'' family are dressed in their finest. The father wears a grey coat and yellow straw hat. He carries a black pipe. The mother wears a tall black hat, red blouse and yellow skirt. The daughter is dressed in black and red, while the baby's clothes are pure white. Photo - courtesy of The Children's Museum of Indianapolis. $15-20

Plate 153 Dutch family. This 5'' set of 4 are dressed in Dutch costumes. The family is blonde. The father and son wear black caps and trousers and red shirts. The mother and daughter wear Dutch caps of white. Their dresses are black, white and turquoise. Photo - courtesy of The Children's Museum of Indianapolis. $15-20

Plate 154 Sailor families. Both sailor families are alike except for size and shape. (Left) This set of three is 6'' tall. The father, mother and child are all dressed in navy and white sailor suits. The father holds a brown pipe in his hand. (Right) All three members of this family are round. The set is 7'' tall with the family dressed in navy and white sailor suits. The father smokes a large brown pipe. $12-18

86

Plate 155 Peasant families. All three peasant families include a father, mother and son. The families represent different costumes from various regions. (Left) This set of three is 6'' tall. The father is dressed in dark blue and red with a black hat. The mother wears a white headpiece, navy blue cape, white apron and pale green skirt. The boy resembles his father in a navy blue coat, black hat and red trousers. (Middle) In this 6½'' set of three, all members are dressed in white with round black hats. The clothing is decorated in geometric patterns of red and blue. (Right) This 5½'' set is known as the Musician or the man from Kielce. The father wears a tall red hat and a long red coat. He carries a brown violin. The mother wears a tall hat and coat of turquoise. The son wears a tall red hat, white shirt and striped trousers. $15-20

Plate 156 Indians and Soldiers. (Left) This Americanized Indian has also been called a Mountain man. The set of three is 7'' tall. The largest figures wears a headdress of feathers and yellow buckskin. The bare-chested middle man wears yellow trousers and a blue loin cloth. The small man wears nothing but a red loin cloth. (Right) This 7½'' soldier set of three is tall and thin. Their uniforms consist of red helmets and jackets, black belts and boots and white trousers. $15-20

Plate 157 The Country Squire and The Baron. Both sets of men are 6½'' tall. (Left) The Country Squire is a set of brunette men with large mustaches. They wear tall black hats, white shirts, red string ties, multicolored striped pants and jackets of orange or green. (Right) The baron is a single man with a large, dark mustache. His tall black hat has three flowers on the front. He wears a white shirt, red string tie, red jacket and sash and navy blue trousers. Inside nests a brown bottle of wine and a silver mug. $15-20

Plate 158 Handpainted eggs (6). The six eggs in this 5½'' set are all handpainted. Each egg is painted a solid color, and then decorated with painted floral designs. Every egg within a set has a different design. The colors used are red, orange, green, yellow, blue and white. $13-18

Plate 159 Wood burned eggs (3). All three of these wood-burned sets contain three eggs. The sets are 3½'' tall. Most of the eggs are left their natural wood tone. Flowers, birds and geometric patterns decorate the surfaces. Accents of red, green and blue paint complete the design. $12-16

Plate 160 Egg with lambs. This 4'' egg houses two white lambs with pink noses. They wear red collars with yellow bells around their necks. The egg is painted in pale green and white. The green represents mountains. White lambs are painted on the egg. Rare $12-20

Plate 161 Egg with owls. Three wise old owls nest inside this 4'' egg. The dark blue egg depicts a brown owl in flight at night. The interior owls are dark brown with large yellow eyes. $14-20

Plate 162 Egg with girl. This lovely 4'' egg holds a single girl. The egg is painted with maidens holding hands around the egg. They are dressed in white blouses, black vests and blue or red skirts and babushkas. The interior doll is a brunette with outstretched arms. She wears a white blouse, black vest and red skirt. Photo - courtesy of The Children's Museum of Indianapolis. $10-15

Plate 163 Nesting Apples. This apple nesting set of three stands 3″ tall. All three apples are yellow and red with brown stems. The largest apple has a green plastic leaf. $8-12

Plate 164 Cider set. The apple in this cider set is 3″ tall. The apple is painted red and yellow with a brown stem. Inside is a set of natural wood dishes painted with white floral designs. $10-15

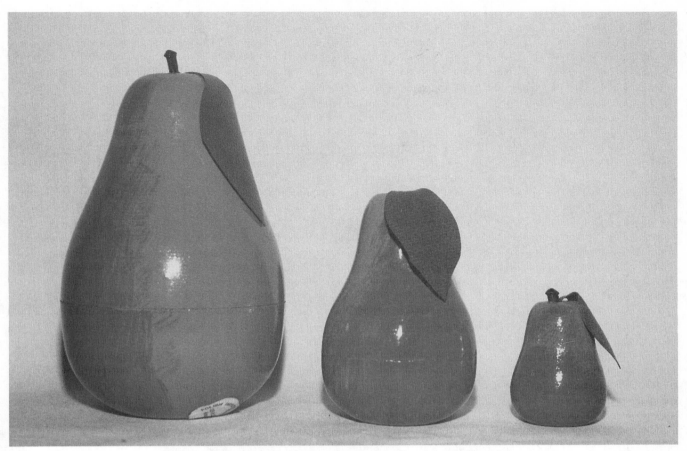

Plate 165 Nesting Pears. The three pears in this 5'' set are painted yellow and red. They have brown plastic stems and green plastic leaves. $8-12

Plate 166 Large mushroom house. The large mushroom house is 5¾'' with a red roof and blue base. A turquoise chimney rises out of the roof and white polka dots decorate the surface. Green grass and flowers decorate the base. Inside the house, two red balls and nine dwarfs are found. Each dwarf wears a different color cap, shirt and pants. Colors include grey, blue, turquoise, red, orange, green and yellow. $18-25

92

Plate 167 Small mushroom house. This 3'' mushroom house is a miniature version of the full size mushroom. It is painted white with a red roof. The roof is decorated with white polka dots. Inside are four white bearded dwarfs. They wear caps, shirts and trousers of red, orange, green, blue, pink, yellow and turquoise. $10-15

Plate 168 White bowling pin. Is there a better place to store a bowling set than in a large bowling pin? This 6'' pin is painted white with red flowers and greenery decorating the surface. Inside are two red wooden balls and nine natural wood pins. Photo - courtesy of The Children's Museum of Indianapolis. Rare. $20-30

LEFT
U.S.S.R., Zagorsk region, Old family set with boys (6). This early 6¼" set of 6 Zagorsk dolls includes 3 boys. Each brown-haired doll has a hand-painted face with simple black features. The women wear babushkas, while the boys are without hats. The boys' clothing is painted yellow, green or red with red string belts. The largest boy wears green mittens. The women are dressed in babushkas, sarafans with straps, long sleeved blouses and aprons. The women's clothing is painted dark blue, yellow, red and orange. The largest lady has simple dot flowers decorating her apron. She carries a brown kerchief bag as well. Like most Zagorsk dolls, they do not carry bouquets. *Rare.* *$50-125.*

BELOW
U.S.S.R., Unknown Soviet regions, Elongated maidens II. The 4 blonde maidens in this old set of 4 stand 4¾" tall. They are dressed in babushkas, blouses, vests and skirts of different muted colors—white, red, tan, blue, yellow and green. *$25-35.*

ABOVE
U.S.S.R., Semenov region, Warriors, and Good Family Man. (Left) The Good Family Man set of 4 is 5" tall. The white-bearded father is dressed in a yellow coat, and red cap trimmed with fingerprinted fur. The mother is a traditional Semenov maiden dressed in a yellow babushka and red dress. The son's red cap and purple trousers accent his natural wood shirt. The tiny daughter is garbed in a red cap and skirt, and a natural wood coat. (Right) This set of 5 warriors is 6½" tall. All 5 wear onion domed, red helmets, purple trousers and yellow tunics with black fingerprint swirls. They have white beards and black eyes. The largest warrior carries a yellow club and red shield. *$12-18.*

LEFT
U.S.S.R., Brest region, Gnomes II. These 7 happy, smiling gnomes are 4½" tall. They are blue-eyed with long white beards and large noses. Each gnome wears a red stocking cap and brown shoes. Their shirts are natural wood with various designs—polka dots, plaid, stars and crosses in assorted colors. They each wear a different color of pants—dark green, turquoise, orange, blue and light green. The gnomes hold various natural items—mushrooms, pinecones, acorns, berries and flowers. *$25-35.*

LEFT
U.S.S.R., Tiraspol, Maidens. There are 6 members in this 6" set. All the maidens have black hair and eyes. They wear yellow babushkas trimmed with red flower buds and greenery. Each of their blouses and aprons are left natural wood with black fingerprint swirls. Their bouquets are made of large red flowers and small blue buds. *$25-30.*

RIGHT
U.S.S.R., Moldavia region, St. Nick or Grandfather Mazay. These two Moldavian sets of old gents are quite similar. Each man has large blue eyes, white eyebrows, mustaches, beards and hair. They wear caps, jackets, black belts, mittens and yellow woven packs filled with orange hearts on their backs. In the large 6" set, the men wear either blue or green jackets and caps. In the small 4¼" set, both men wear green caps and mittens, and red coats. The smallest figure is a grey hare. *$15-25.*

BELOW
U.S.S.R., Semenov region, 8" Maiden and male bottle holders. Dressed in traditional Semenov colors—red, yellow and black. The male has orange hair and a red belt. Both dolls are painted with bright roses of red, pink, yellow and orange. *$18-25 each.*

ABOVE
U.S.S.R., Polkhov Maiden, Thin maidens with baskets. The 3 dolls in this 6⅛" set have a most unusual shape. The curly-haired dolls wear yellow bonnets with a Polkh flower, red and turquoise dresses and natural wood pinafores. Simple flowers of red, pink, yellow and blue decorate the dolls. These dolls are unusual for Polkh maidens because they have arms. Each maiden carries a yellow basket. *$17-20.*

RIGHT
U.S.S.R., Southern regions, Aiguel sets of males & maidens. Oriental influence. Both sets open at the bottom. The 3¾" set of males is painted in black, yellow, red and dark green. Their black hair is covered by elaborate hoods with floral patterns down the back. They wear natural wood shirts and black or green jackets. The 3" female set is painted red, yellow, black, green and natural wood. The largest doll wears a long red babushka with floral patterns of yellow and natural wood. She wears large white beads and a black dress. The two smaller maidens wear red caps and long red veils decorated with red and yellow ball fringe. Their coats are painted green, red and natural wood tones. The maidens have black hair. *Rare. $30-50.*

LEFT
U.S.S.R., Brest region, Fisherman box and Woodcutters. (Left) The fisherman is a single, round headed box. He stands 6¾" tall as one of the largest Brest pieces. The balding man has orange hair, a beard and mustache. He is dressed in a natural wood shirt with red and black geometric trim. He wears a brown vest with a blue band, and blue trousers. He holds a large orange fish and a black fishing net. (Right) The 5½" set of woodcutters has pointed heads. The blue-eyed men have orange hair, beards and mustaches. They wear natural wood shirts trimmed with geometric bands of red and black patterns. Each man wears grey and yellow striped trousers. They hold various tools painted brown and grey. *$12-24.*

LEFT
U.S.S.R., Kalinin region, 3 maidens & roly poly maiden. (Left) The 3 maidens in this 4½" set are tall and thin. The geometric patterns are wood-burned lines. They wear clothing of natural wood tones, red and black. (Right) This single roly poly is short and fat at 3" tall. The bottom is weighted. The blue-eyed blonde is dressed in a green babushka, red dress and pink beads. Her clothing has been delineated with wood-burned lines. *$9-12.*

ABOVE
U.S.S.R., Brest region, Solid maidens. These 3 blonde, blue-eyed, solid maidens range in size from 2-4" tall. The 3 dolls wear red babushkas trimmed in brown or orange. The largest doll is dressed in a natural wood vest and apron with red and black trim. Her vest has orange and her skirt is green, grey and blue stripes. She holds a single red flower in her hands. The two small dolls have natural wood dresses with round black aprons. The aprons are decorated with red water lilies. The smallest doll is a Christmas tree ornament. *$3-8.*

RIGHT
U.S.S.R., Brest region, Christmas maidens. All 7 dolls are dressed alike in this 5½" set. The orange-haired dolls have rounded heads and big blue eyes. The blouses and aprons are natural wood with red and black trim. The maidens wear red babushkas, dark green curved vests, and green and natural wood plaid skirts. *$35-40.*

LEFT

U.S.S.R., Ukraine region, Bullet & conical maidens. 2 most common shapes. (Left) This 3¼" set is bullet-shaped. Each doll has a different hair color—brown, black and tan. They wear geometric patterns on their blouses, babushkas, aprons and skirts. The largest doll has 2 yellow birds painted on the back of her babushka. Colors used are black, brown, tan, yellow, orange, green and maroon. (Right) This 2¾" set is conical or egg-shaped inside with either black or brown hair. The dolls wear white blouses with orange and red patterns, black or dark brown vests, and striped skirts of green or red. Floral patterns are painted on their yellow and green babushkas. The largest doll carries a bouquet of red flowers and has a brown bird painted on the back of her scarf. The middle doll carries a book. *$14-20.*

ABOVE

Japan, Elaborate kokeshi sets. These lovely sets of 3 are 4½" tall. The heads are separate from the bodies and are movable. These sets are very unusual for Japanese kokeshi because they mix male and female dolls within the same set. Very elaborate painting is done on all six dolls. The two largest males are bald and the rest of the dolls have black hair. Their rich clothing is painted in many colors of pale blue, turquoise, gold, pink, red, white, silver, black, and royal blue. *$15-25 pair.*

ABOVE

Japan, Kokeshi maiden boxes. The narrow tube kokeshi maidens are from the late 1950's-early 1960's. When you unscrew their bases, a paper message can be rolled up and inserted inside the doll. The doll on the left is 3½" tall. She has black hair and eyes. Her body is natural wood with dots of green, orange, red and white. The doll on the right is 4½" tall with black hair. Her natural wood body is decorated with red and purple flowers. The wide doll in the middle is a 3¾" box. She opens at the neck to hold objects. She has pink skin, black hair and a pale blue kimono. She holds a red fan in her hand. *$5-20.*

BELOW

Poland, Peasant families. All 3 peasant families include a father, mother and son. The families represent different costumes from various regions. (Left) This set of 3 is 6" tall. The father is dressed in dark blue and red with a black hat. The mother wears a white headpiece, navy blue cape, white apron, and pale green skirt. The boy resembles his father in a navy blue coat, black hat and red trousers. (Middle) In this 6½" set of 3, all members are dressed in white with round black hats. The clothing is decorated in geometric patterns of red and blue. (Right) This 5½" set is known as the Musician or the man from Kielce. The father wears a tall red hat and a long red coat. He carries a brown violin. The mother wears a tall hat and coat of turquoise. The son wears a tall red hat, white shirt and striped trousers. *$15-20.*

ABOVE

Taiwan, Cat families by Midwest Importers of Cannon Falls. These 5¼" sets of tan, grey and yellow cats nest separately as male and female families. The female cats are dressed in red and yellow skirts and blouses. The male cats wear shirts and trousers of white, blue, yellow and red. *$10-15.*

LEFT
Poland, Zakopane maidens, red & natural. Both of these 3½" sets of maidens are alike except they have clothing color differences. All the maidens from the Zakopane region have black hair. These sets of 6 have blue eyes. The dolls on the left wear red dresses and green babushkas. The dolls on the right are dressed in natural wood dresses with multi-colored stripes. Their babushkas are red. *$16-25.*

RIGHT
Poland, Nowysacz maidens (Black hair) in green babushka. In this lovely set of 5, the dolls have full eyes and lashes. The set is 4" tall with matching dolls. Each black haired doll wears a green babushka, yellow vest, red skirt, white blouse and apron. The apron has elaborate fringe around the border. The dolls carry bouquets of red, blue and white flowers. (5) *$12-18.*

LEFT
Poland, Nowysacz maidens (Black hair) in white babushka (4). Four maidens nest in this 3¼" set. The maidens wear white babushkas with tiny red flowers decorating the surface. Their aprons and blouses are also white. Navy blue jackets with red trim and red skirts complete their clothing. The black-haired dolls hold their natural wood hands at their waist. *$10-15.*

RIGHT
Poland, Dutch maidens. This large set of 6 represents Dutch girls in regional costumes. All but the baby have brown hair; she is a blonde. In this 7" set, the maidens wear either dutch caps or babushkas of white, blue or yellow. They wear skirts, aprons, blouses and vests in assorted colors — red, yellow, blue, white, black, and turquoise. Photo—courtesy of The Children's Museum of Indianapolis. *$25-35.*

RIGHT
China, The Greatest Show by Authentic Models Holland. This 5½" circus set of 5 begins with either a grey, white or tan elephant. The clown wears red pants, bow tie and cap, and a yellow jacket. The strongman is dressed in pale blue and white. The highwire performer is wearing red with a yellow umbrella. The last piece in the set is a horn player. In some sets the smallest piece is a tan monkey and in others, it is a person dressed in blue and white. *$19-27.*

LEFT
China, 5 Fishermen by Authentic Models Holland. This 5½" set of 5 fishermen has all similar men in turquoise raingear. Each man holds a rope which has been tied in different knots. *$19-27.*

RIGHT
China, Dutch Girls by Authentic Models Holland. This set of 5 is described as farmer and fishing village Dutch girls by the manufacturer. The 5½" dolls are dressed in national dresses of Holland. The clothing colors used are bright yellows, reds, blues, whites and black. Each girl wears yellow wooden shoes. *Rare. $25-30.*

LEFT
China, Monkey Wisdom by Authentic Models Holland. This set of 5 monkeys is 5½" tall. The largest is a black gorilla daddy holding a black baby. Mama is tan in a green dress holding a tan infant. A black monkey dressed in pink holds another black baby. The last two chimps are tan and white. *$19-27.*

LEFT
China, Santa Claus by Authentic Models Holland. Jolly old St. Nick and his helpers are 5½" tall. This set of 5 starts with Santa dressed in traditional colors of red and white. Next is a tan reindeer. The last three are elves also dressed in red and white. *$19-27.*

LEFT
India, 3 Maharani by Kubla Crafts. This lovely set of 3 ladies is 5½" tall. The natural wood faces of the women are accented with black hair and eyes. They wear green blouses and red veils and saris. The veils and saris are delicately painted in yellow with simple patterns. *$15-20.*

RIGHT
India, 3 Scarecrows by Kubla Crafts. The scarecrow set of 3 has a most unusual shape. The dolls open at the neckline. The set is 5½" tall. The scarecrows have natural wood faces with stringy brown hair. Their old floppy hats are dark brown with yellow patches, and yellow rope bands. They wear red shirts, grey shoes, and black trousers. The trousers are patched with red and yellow geometric shapes. *$15-20.*

RIGHT
India, 5 Clowns by Kubla Crafts. The circus clown set of 5 dolls is 5½" tall. The orange-haired fellows have natural wood faces, green shirts and red trousers. Their large bow ties are striped with red and green. *$15-20.*

RIGHT
India, Gypsy Family by Authentic Models Holland. This gypsy family of 5 is 6" tall. They appear quite rugged with dark skin tones, black hair and eyes. The two largest figures are men dressed in white shirts and dark trousers. The largest man holds a guitar. The largest girl wears a tan blouse and dark skirt. The two small girls wear polka dot dresses—one white and the other red. *Rare. $30-$35.*

LEFT
India, 5 Fishermen by Kubla Crafts. This set of 5 fishermen is 5½" tall. They are painted with dark turquoise raingear. They have long, narrow faces with large noses. Their white beards are scantily painted. All 5 fishermen hold ropes knotted in different ways. *$15-20.*

RIGHT
India, 5 Wizard of Oz by Kubla Crafts. Follow the yellow brick road with this 5 piece set. This 5½" set includes Dorothy, the scarecrow, the cowardly lion, the tin man and little Toto. Dorothy is a brown-haired beauty with a yellow blouse, blue jumper, white plaid apron and ruby slippers. She holds a woven basket in her hands. The scarecrow has a yellow face and dark brown clothing. The lion is painted in several hues of tan. The tin man is grey and Toto, the dog, is dark brown. *$15-20.*

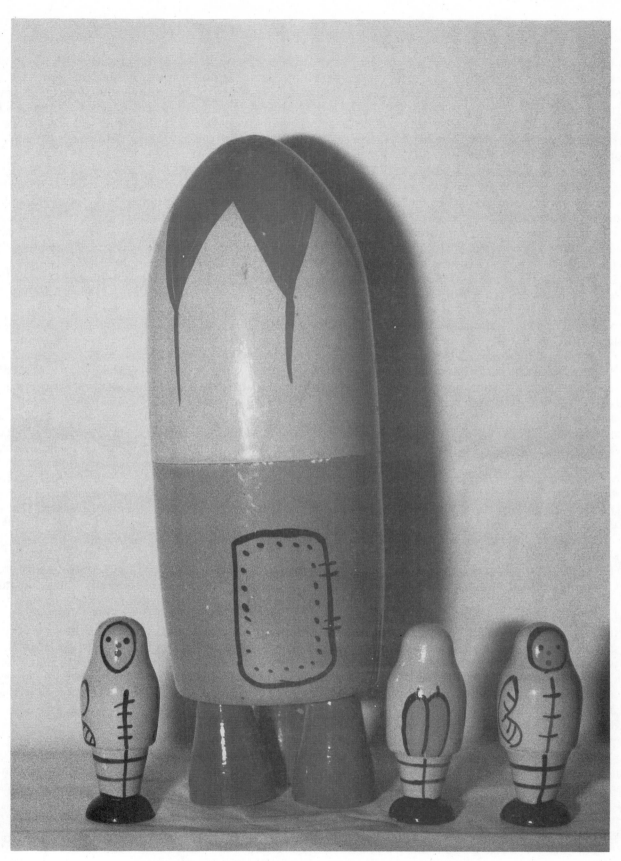

Plate 169 Rocket ship with cosmonauts. This most unusual nesting set is about 6'' tall. The rocket is painted red, white and turquoise. A door is painted on the side. Inside are three cosmonauts dressed in grey with blue air tanks on their backs. Rare. $20-30

JAPAN

The Japanese people are the most enthusiastic doll collectors on earth. No other country reflects their culture so successfully through the dolls they create. Japan has a long history of doll and toy making that dates back to 2000 B.C. Japanese folk art, which includes doll making, is alive and thriving today. Industrialization developed on the island country during this century. Despite that, the arts flourish. In Japan, there are annual, national doll festivals held for both girls and boys. Japanese artists skillfully create many types of folk dolls. Nesting dolls, whose concept was borrowed from the Chinese, are a minor variety. Nevertheless, the nesting dolls that are made frequently are quite popular in both Japan and abroad.

The nesting dolls still excite young and old as their inner secrets are revealed. The kokeshi is a representative folk toy. Most Japanese nesting sets have evolved from the kokeshi. The kokeshi were originally made in northeastern Japan in the Tohoku region, Miyagi Prefecture. Later the quaint dolls became popular as travel souvenirs in all parts of the country. Today the classic kokeshi remain the best known and most popular of the Japanese wooden dolls.

Kokeshi dolls possess a very distinct and yet simple form. Their limbless bodies are constructed of one cylindrical piece of wood that meets a disproportionately large, round, moveable, wooden head. They are lathe made of hard grained woods and generally adorned with animated hand painted clothing or floral designs.

Typically, kokeshi are made as children's toys. However, they are also offered by childless wives as good luck charms to bring children. Huge numbers of kokeshi in various styles have been exported to the United States both as playthings for children and as aesthetic expressions of the Japanese culture.

There are several sets of kokeshi nesting dolls that have imitated the traditional solid kokeshis. The nesting sets emphasize fertility even more dramatically. These sets are often representative of families. Sets of three are the most common including an infant, a child and an adult. The gender of the dolls in a set is almost always the same. Frequently you can purchase two sets sold as a complete family unit. The sets contain a mother, daughter, and an infant daughter, as well as a father, son and an infant son. Sets of two are manufactured with an adult and child. Larger sets of four or more are manufactured, yets sets of three are usually imported and sold in the United States.

The kokeshi nesting dolls have the same large, moveable heads as their original counterparts. They are merely hollow inside to allow the smaller dolls to nest. Most often, the female dolls are painted in different hues of red clothing. The men are garbed in shades of green or blue. These small nesting sets are inexpensive and sold as souvenirs.

A second type of Japanese nesting dolls are more simple in shape than the kokeshi. These dolls are one hollow piece without a separate moveable head. Their shape resembles a bullet. Most of these sets portray specific characters. Some sets are made for an international market and are exported. The figures include black-helmeted British soldiers, eskimos, American Indians complete with feather headdresses and Eastern Indian Maharani women. These figures do not represent Japanese culture. Other sets do reflect the charm and ethnicity of Japan. The Daruma sets and the Fukurokuju, or Seven gods of happiness are two dominant examples. Older sets of the "immortals" and fierce Japanese warriors can be found.

The Daruma or tumbling doll is one of the oldest and most common folk toys of Japan. Daruma is more known in Japan than in the West, unlike the popular kokeshi. The Daruma dolls are also used as good luck charms. These dolls are bought by the Japanese people on the first day of the new year to insure good fortune for the entire year to come.

Daruma is also known as Bodhidharma, an Indian monk or saint. He is credited with having brought Zen Buddhism to China. According to legend, after ten years of constant prayer and meditation, Daruma's limbs withered away. As a result of this legend, the dolls are always portrayed without arms or legs. Ten years of meditation caused Daruma's head to grow upwards as well. Most often, Daruma is shaped like an egg. Frequently he is weighted so that he always swings back to an upright position. The ability to "come out on top" in all circumstances accounts for its value as a lucky charm.

Ordinarily the Daruma is in the form of a male figure. There is one region in Japan that makes female Darumas from paper mache. When depicted as a male, Daruma usually has a white face and black hair. On occasion, his eyes are also painted black. In vivid contrast, Daruma's body and head are frequently painted bright red or orange.

Sometimes Darumas are made with the eyes left unpainted. This is done so that the owner can paint in one eye and then the other eye, if his wishes are granted through Daruma's intercession. When both eyes are painted in, Daruma figures can be taken to a Buddhist temple as an offering.

As nesting dolls, the Darumas are hollow with the smaller dolls inside. They are painted red with natural wood faces, fierce expressions and black eyes. The dolls in one set alternate colors – red and natural wood tones. The smallest doll in the set of five is a red shape with two black dot eyes. There is a lacquered set that includes a pair of dice as the smallest figures inside a very fat Daruma. This set is a gambling game. The lacquer is a very dark red. The Daruma gambling set is considered to be a toy and not used as a good luck charm. A third set is made with a hollow Daruma. When you unscrew his base, seven, tiny, solid Darumas fit unnested inside. This Daruma also possesses protruding eyes that emphasize his function as a good luck piece. The final Daruma included here is a rare example of a female Daruma. She is a wooden set of four nested dolls. The Darumas are identical, except for size. She exhibits the red and white colors of her male counterparts.

The Fukurokuju, or Seven gods of happiness are Shinto gods. Shintoism, Japan's native religion, is practiced only in Japan. It is a form of nature worship; its gods are those of the forests, waterfalls, rivers and the sea. Heroes of the past are also included as Shinto gods. The seven nesting dolls represent the happy dieties. They bring joy to all who unnest them. The Seven gods are very simple in form, diminishing in size to 1/16''. The Fukurokuju are very infrequently found in the United States. They are much more available in Japan, as the Darumas are.

Nested novelty toys are a third type of Japanese folk art. They are not traditional, Japanese dolls. Many sets are made as inexpensive children's trinkets, manufactured for export. It is possible to purchase a set of five nested houses, a Noah's ark with animals, five different fruit sets and four egg sets. Dogs, rabbits, mushroom houses with Snow White and the seven dwarfs, soldiers, policemen, maidens with tea sets inside, and maiden crayon containers have also been produced as children's toys. These items are not dolls, but often nesting doll collectors include them in their collections.

The set of five houses is built with pastel colors of inlaid wood in geometric patterns. As the houses decrease in size, the detail diminishes. Each roof has a different pastel color. The houses do possess a certain charm in their simplicity.

Noah's ark is a crude and simple container that houses small, wooden animals. The roof of the ark opens to reveal the hollow space below. Jigsaw cut, flat animals fill up the void of the ark. There is also a figure of Noah and his wife. The ark qualifies as a nested set because items fit inside the larger container.

Fruit sets are manufactured in Japan, Taiwan and Poland. Japan has created nested pineapples, peaches, pears and apples. The pear sets contain a peach, a plum and a cherry. Many apple tea nesting sets are produced. Similar cider sets are also made in Poland and Taiwan. All the ciders are large apples with small wooden dishes inside. Some sets are more elaborate then others. The Japanese set is a miniature. It is quite small, simple and inexpensive. The miniature cider sets are found in abundance here in the U.S.A. A second Japanese apple surprisingly contains solid, wooden pigs. This miniature apple is quite unique.

Four egg sets are made in Japan. The first set is a tiny miniature egg with a tiny baby inside. The baby is dressed in white. The second set addresses the question, ''Which came first, the chicken or the egg?''. This older set begins with a chicken. It alternates chickens and eggs in a charming toy. What child would not be fascinated? A newer version of the chicken and egg theme was made. This set contained three, small, yellow and red chickens with a tiny egg inside. A fourth set of eggs simply nests striped eggs.

The dogs, rabbits, mushroom house, soldiers, policemen, and maidens were made earlier in this century. They were quite popular imports but are less available today.

Japan's rich folk art tradition continues to flourish. Probably no other country can rival the arts of Japan. Artists create lovely dolls reflecting this complex culture. Perhaps nesting dolls will gain more prominance in the field of Japanese dolls. For today, we will enjoy the sets that are made and available to us here in America.

Plate 170 Elaborate kokeshi sets. These lovely sets of three are 4½'' tall. The heads are separate from the bodies and are movable. THese sets are very unusual for Japanese kokeshi because they mix male and female dolls within the same set. Very elaborate painting is done on all six dolls. The two largest males are bald and the rest of the dolls have black hair. Their rich clothing is painted in many colors of pale blue, turquoise, gold, pink, red, white, silver, black and royal blue. $15-25 pair

Plate 171 Small kokeshi sets, maidens and males. These four sets of kokeshi nesting dolls are common. The largest dolls are 3'' tall. All of the figures have black hair and eyes and wobble heads. The female sets are dressed in shades of red, pink and blues. The males are dressed in shades of green and brown. $10-15 pair

Plate 172 Kokeshi maidens. This 5'' set of three kokeshi maidens is unique because it is matte finished. The black-haired ladies wear red caps. Their kimonos are orange, pink green, red and blue. $10-15

97

Plate 173 Small Kokeshi sets (3, 2, 2). (Left) This 3¼'' set of three female kokeshi is painted with much detail. They have black hair and red caps. The lovely kimonos are painted pink, red, yellow and turquoise. (Right) These two sets of 2¼'' kokeshi dolls are a pair. The female set of two is dressed in reds, while the male set of two is dressed in blue. $5-15

Plate 174 Kokeshi maiden boxes. The narrow tube kokeshi maidens are from the late 1950's-early 1960's. When you unscrew their bases, a paper message can be rolled up and inserted inside the doll. The doll on the left is 3½'' tall. She has black hair and eyes. Her body is natural wood with dots of green, orange, red and white. THe doll on the right is 4½'' tall with black hair. Her natural wood body is decorated with red and purple flowers. The wide doll in the middle is a 3¾'' box. She opens at the neck to hold objects. She has pink skin, black hair and a pale blue kimono. She holds a red fan in her hand. $5-20

Plate 175 Black helmeted British soldiers. This 4'' set of two had at least one more piece at one time. They open at the base of their tall black helmets. Large yellow feathers and insignia are painted on the front of the helmets. They have pink faces and black facial features. The uniforms have red jackets, green pants and black shoes. $5-20

Plate 176 Eskimo, Indian and Maharani. All three of these sets are 3½'' tall and incomplete. The Eskimo on the left is dressed in red and blue with a black hood. The American Indian in the middle wears a red and black headdress with 15 black feathers. The Indian also wears blue and red. The Maharani Indian women is a set of four. At one time, it was a larger set. The bottoms are likewise missing. They are dressed in blue and red. All the figures in these sets have black hair and facial features. $5-20

Plate 177 Warriors & Immortals. (Left) This fierce set of 4½″ warriors once held more than its current three men. They are very elaborately painted with great detail. The beards are black and most of the outlining is also black. Other muted colors are used in shades of red, silver, blue, yellow and green. (Right) This 4¼″ set of immortals is complete with four men. The largest god has a very elongated head of natural wood. They are painted with great detail in muted shades of red, black, white, purple and green. $10-20

Plate 178 Daruma – alternating colors. This matte finished Daruma of five is 2¼″ tall. All but the smallest piece have natural wood faces with fierce expressions. They have black wispy beards and black facial features. The largest, middle and smallest dolls have red clothing with accents of black. The other two dolls are entirely natural wood. The smallest doll is all red. $10-17

Plate 179 Daruma – lacquered dice game. This 3″ unusual set of three Darumas is a dice game. All three men have tan faces, large black mustaches and black facial features. They are dressed in dark maroon. Inside the smallest doll is a maroon die. $8-15

100

Plate 180 Daruma – inside of dice game. Both the lids and bottoms of the Darumas are used in this dice game. Six different face masks are painted on the insides of these maroon pieces. The largest mask is a tan old man with a long white beard. A drawing of five on the die is next to the mask. A pink man with a large nose is painted next with a die of four. A green devil mask and the die of three are next. A tan face with black hair and the die of two follows. A pink devil mask and the die one is the last mask. A gold musical note fills the last lid. $8-15

Plate 181 Daruma – hollow with solid figures inside. This miniature orange Daruma is about 2″ tall. He has a natural wood face with fierce black facial features. His clothing is orange with accents of white and gold. He opens at his base. Inside are seven ½″ miniatures of the large Daruma. $5-15

Plate 182 Daruma - Female. This 2″ female Daruma is a lovely set of four. They have natural wood faces with delicate black facial features. The female Darumas have jet black hair. Their clothing is bright red with white accents and gold writing on the front. Photo - courtesy of The Children's Museum of Indianapolis. $5-15

Plate 183 Fukurokuju or seven immortals. Fukurokuju stands 3¼″ tall as a set of seven. The largest piece has an elongated head of natural wood. He has black facial features, mustache and beard. He is colorfully dressed in yellow, green, red and blue. The interior dolls are varnished and much simpler. They are primarily natural wood tones with black details. Red, yellow, purple, pink and green are used to add color to these smaller pieces. $12-18

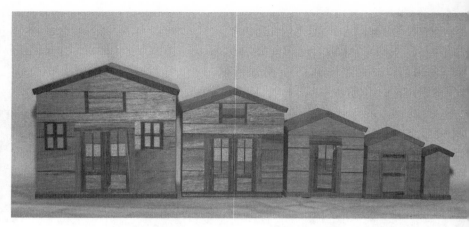

Plate 184 Miniature immortals. This minute ½'' set of three is probably from a larger set. The unvarnished figures are primari-ly natural wood with details painted in black. The two largest men wear black caps. Touches of color add details – pink, yellow, red and blue. The smallest doll is merely a piece of unpainted wood. $2-7

Plate 185 Inlaid houses. These wooden inlaid houses are almost 3'' tall. The five houses split at the roof line. Each house has a different color roof – red, blue, green and orange. The same four colors are used on the front of the tan houses in an inlay of wood. The houses have doors and windows. Detail diminishes as the houses decrease in size. $10-15

Plate 186 Noah's Ark and miniature cider set. (Left) The wooden ark is 3½'' tall and 5½'' long. The red roof opens to house flat wooden animals and Noah and his wife. The natural wood ark has black wooden portals and a deck. The animals are yellow, tan, blue, brown pairs. (Right) This tiny red apple including the black stem is only 1¾'' tall. Inside is a complete tea set made of natural wood with red and green details. $3-5

Plate 187 Pineapples. Five pieces of fruit are in this 4'' set. The largest piece is a yellow and red pineapple with a green stem. Inside the four pieces of fruit are nondescript and red. $5-20

Plate 188 Pear, peach, plum and cherry. All four pieces of fruit in this 4″ set are different. The yellow and red pear has a green stem and leaf. The yellow and red peach also has a green leaf. The plum is dark purple with a green leaf. The red cherry is simple and small. $5-20

Plate 189 Apple with solid pigs. This 2″ red and yellow apple with a black stem opens to hold four tiny, solid pink pigs. $5-20

Plate 190 Miniature egg with baby. This tiny, turquoise egg is only 1¼″ tall. It is decorated with yellow centered pink flowers and greenery. Inside nests a ¾″ baby. The bald baby has a flesh tone head with two black eyes. The bunting is white with a red tie. $1-5

Plate 191 Large chicken and egg set. This 5'' set of five chickens and eggs had at least one more piece at one time. The largest chicken has a protruding beak and red comb. All three chickens have yellow bodies with orange eyes and red wings. The largest egg is all natural wood. The smaller egg is natural wood with multi-color stripes. $5-20

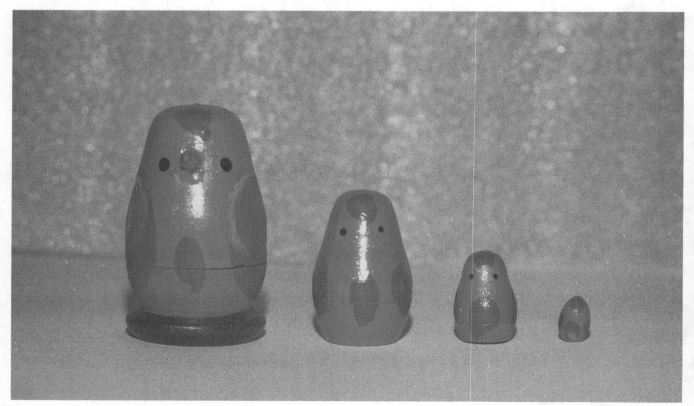

Plate 192 Small chicken set. This 2'' set of four chickens is very simple in form with a protruding beak. The chicks have yellow bodies, red wings and combs and black eyes. Photo - courtesy of The Children's Museum of Indianapolis. $5-20

Plate 193 Egg and duck set. Seven pieces make up this 1½'' nesting egg set. The largest egg is all natural wood with a painted red flower on the front. A solid yellow and then a solid red egg comes next. Two multi-colored eggs follow. Two, tiny, solid, yellow ducks with orange feet complete the set. $5-20

Plate 194 Dogs. Four dogs make up this 1¾'' set. Each dog is simple in form with beige fur. They have black ears, eyebrows, eyes and mouths. The only color is on their red noses. $5-10

Plate 195 Rabbit family. This bunny family of three stands 3½'' tall. The largest rabbit is missing dowel ears. The smaller rabbits have black painted ears. They are painted a pale brown with large noses and black eyes. The clothing consists of pale blue shirts, red pants, black shoes and black belts. $5-10

106

Plate 196 Mushroom house with Snow White and seven dwarfs (front). This 5'' set of 10 includes Snow White, 7 dwarfs and a wolf. The mushroom house is white with a red roof, black chimney, green grass, brown door and green shutters. The pink faced dwarfs wear red caps and shirts, yellow trousers and black shoes. Snow White is garbed in a pink dress. The wolf is tan with a yellow shirt and blue slacks. $10-15

Plate 197 Mushroom house with Snow White and seven dwarfs (rear). The rear of this 5'' mushroom house is decorated by a green and brown fir tree. A large black spider has spun a web across the back of the house. $10-15

107

Plate 198 Soldiers (5). Five soldiers make up this 8'' set. The largest soldier has movable arms and a protruding nose. They are all dressed in the same uniforms. The helmets and shoes are black. The jackets are red and the belts are white. Blue slacks match their blue eyes. $10-20

Plate 199 Policemen (5). Five policemen stand at attention in this 8″ set. The captain has a protruding red nose and movable arms. The entire group wears uniforms of blue with black belts and shoes. The blue helmets have a gold dot in front to match their buttons. $10-20

109

Plate 200 Maiden tea set and Maiden crayon box. These two sets are very nice. The girl on the left opens at the bottom. Her base becomes a natural wood table. Inside is a complete wooden blue tea set and two blue chairs. Both maidens have movable arms and heads. The girl on the right opens at the waist to hold a set of crayons. The maidens have flesh tone skin, brown hair, blue eyes and pink cheeks. They wear beige caps, white blouses and aprons, black vests and either red or green skirts. $10-20 each

INDIA

India is a country rich in culture and artistic tradition. Many of the Indian arts are quite elegant and decorative. The Indians have a long history of folk art as well. Indian artists are well known for their wood and stone carvings. Lovely balsa wood figures and other dolls in traditional costumes are also produced. India has distinguished herself in the world of dolls. However, nesting dolls are not her specialty.

The production of nesting dolls in India is a relatively new craft. An Indian importer from Kubla Crafts recently revealed the Soviet government has set up an exchange program with India. Russian artists have been sent to India where they are instructing local craftsmen in the art of lathe turning wood to produce nesting doll sets. The Russian artisans are also teaching the Indians to paint and lacquer the dolls, package them and export them to the U.S. and Europe. In return, the Indian people are greatly encouraged to spend their new-found revenue on Russian merchandise. The money acquired from the doll sales has been a welcome addition to many Indian homes. As the Soviet artists are the ''experts,'' this exchange program is upgrading the quality of the Indian products.

The earliest Indian made nesting sets were often ill-fitted, poorly painted and sometimes mildewed. The mildew was caused by green and unseasoned wood being used for turning. Also it resulted from the dolls being wrapped in plastic before the paint was completely dried. Often the paint would also peel. These problems rarely occur now that the exchange program has increased the sophistication of their work.

At least three U.S. companies import and sell Indian nesting dolls. Authentic Models Holland (U.S.A.), (see chapter on China), Kubla Crafts and B. Shackman & Co. sell the sets to retailers. There are many one-of-a-kind sets imported by small firms as well. The Indian nesting sets are becoming much more available here than ever before.

Indian nesting sets have many themes and styles. Most often the sets include three or five dolls. Sets of two, four and six are also manufactured. In early Kubla Craft sets, three pieces were included in each group. After 1985, Kubla Craft sets contained five pieces. Nesting dolls depicting bears, cats, clowns and Santas were made in both sets of three and five.

The Indians produce many animal sets. Lions, tigers, bears, cats, monkeys and penguins are made. In 1985, Kubla Crafts added three new sets to their line of ten, increasing it to thirteen. The new sets include a fat bullfrog and a roly-poly penguin. In 1987, the frog and penguin underwent stylistic changes. Both sets of figures were made thinner. The frog now has larger hands and feet with purple accents. The penguin has been black and white. The two new verisons are painted navy blue and white. Three lion sets and three different bear sets are made. With the new Kubla Craft roly-poly and navy blue penguins, there are now four penguin sets made, each quite different from the other.

India manufactures at least four known soldier sets. One set, the Patriot, by Kubla Crafts, is also known as the English Duke or Lord Nelson. The Patriot is missing a hand, just as the real Lord Nelson was handless. Another human theme created is Santa Claus. At first, Kubla Crafts produced a Santa set of three. In 1985. a revised Santa set of five was made available. The new Santa is the same as the three piece version with two additional smaller dolls. A third set of Santa nesting dolls is also made in India. On these Santas, ''Merry Xmas'' is painted on their backs.

The Kubla Crafts line includes two clowns, a scarecrow and a pirate. In 1986, Kubla Crafts produced a set of five grey bearded fishermen. These rope holding fishermen are extraordinarily similar to Authentic Models Holland's white bearded fishermen, made both in India and China. Authentic Models Holland first produced nesting dolls in India. After a fire, the company moved production to China. The Indian fishermen were dark turquoise, while the Chinese version is much lighter. The Kubla Craft copy is colored like the Indian set by Authentic Models Holland. There are now three versions of this fishermen. Prior to the fire, Authentic Models Holland manufactured four sets in India, a fisherman, two versions of a sheik, an eskimo family and a gypsy family. The sheik and gypsy family are no longer manufactured. The gypsy family was a very limited series; only 66 sets were made. The fisherman and eskimo are now manufactured in China.

In 1987, a Sea Captain and the Wizard of Oz set were added to the expanding line of Kubla Crafts offerings. The Sea Captain figures are all alike with only diminishing sizes. However, the Wizard of Oz set is quite different with Dorothy, the scarecrow, the lion, the tinman and finally, little Toto. The Wizard of Oz set is a must for collectors.

Often a country reflects its culture in a style of dress and ethnicity. India produces at least four nesting sets that are examples of her people. The largest set consists of six women dressed in the traditional sari. The set was sold in a woven reed basket, complete with a lid. The dolls wear hues of green, red and orange. The women are identical except for their diminishing sizes. These dolls are not of the highest quality, but they do have charm. A modern variation of this set was made. Instead of wearing the traditional sari, the women wear long red dresses, loose, uncovered flowing hair and sunglasses. It is a satirical interpretation of the traditional doll.

Another modern Indian family of four is manufactured wearing red or green clothing. The father's head wobbles on a spring. This set is crudely made and is very inexpensive. Yet it, too, has a positive charm.

The most lovely set and best example of Indian people is the "Maharani" of Kubla Crafts. It is a set of three women wearing neat saris. The set is well made, painted and lacquered with great care and attention to detail. This set is also the most expensive of the four native Indian sets.

Indian artists have copied exact duplicates of Russian pieces. You can purchase "Semenov" maidens and "Brest Region" black lacquered lady sets made in India. The untrained eye can easily be fooled by these copies. If you are collecting only Russian sets, be sure to check the labels and markings usually found on the bottom. Indian "Black Lacquered" sets have smaller faces, rounded ties on their babushkas and white accents painted on their babushkas. The Indian "Semenov" maidens have much simpler eyes and lips then their Russian prototypes. Their babushkas are decorated with red dots. The Indian dolls hold a single pink flower. Most Russian Semenov carry bouquets. It is important to compare an original with a copy to become familiar with their stylistic differences.

With the Soviet/Indian exchange program working, it is likely that greater numbers of Indian sets will be produced and imported. There is a definite market for them here in America, especially with their many interesting and varied themes.

Plate 201 Lions by B. Shackman & Co. Both sets of three lions are 5" tall. (Left) In this set, the lions are tan. They wear dark brown scarves on their heads. (Right) In this set, the tan lions have red spots on their fur. The wear red capes over their heads and backs.　　　$10-15

112

Plate 202 Red lions. This set of four lions are 3¼'' tall. These fierce lions are red with black manes, white ears and teeth. $15-20

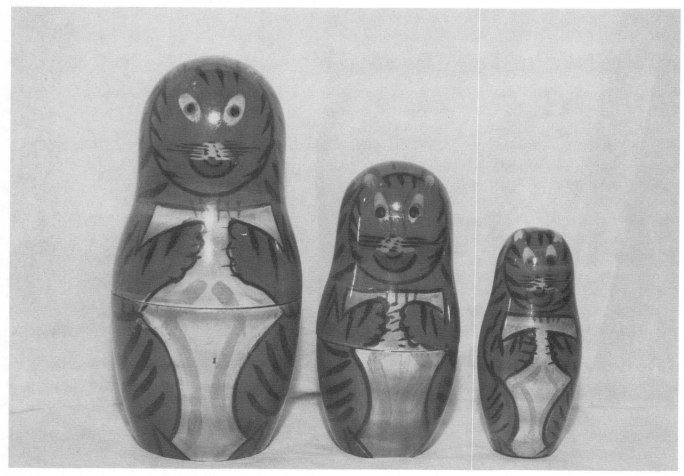

Plate 203 Tigers by B. Shackman & Co. This 5'' set of three tigers are painted orange with black stripes. All three have beige stomachs. $10-15

113

Plate 204 Five cats by Kubla Crafts. This set of 5''
orange cats wear green collars and red tags. All five
are alike with yellow eyes, ears and breasts. $15-20

Plate 205 Three Bears I by B. Shackman & Co. The three bears in this
5'' set are very somber. They have dark brown fur. The papa bear wears
a red cape, while mama wears a yellow bonnet and green dress. Baby
wears nothing but his brown fur. $10-15

Plate 206 Three Bears II by B. Shackman & Co. The three bears in this 5″ set are a happy trio. They have warm brown fur. Papa and baby wear yellow vests and red bowties. Mama matches with a yellow apron and red tie. $10-15

Plate 207 Three Teddy bears by Kubla Crafts. This cuddly trio wear purple ribbons around their necks. The 5½″ set has two-tone tan fur and black eyes. $12-15

Plate 208 Five Teddy bears by Kubla Crafts. This cuddly 5½'' set of five bears wear purple ribbons around their necks. They have tan fur and beige bellies with black eyes. $15-20

Plate 209 Three monkeys. This set of three banana munching monekys is 5'' tall. They have dark brown fur, yellow stomachs and orange faces. They have large red mouths and black eyes. $15-20

Plate 210 Three Penguins by B. Shackman & Co. This trio is a set of black and white birds. They are 5'' tall with red lips, eyes and bowties.
$10-15

Plate 211 Five Black & White Penguins by Kubla Crafts. This 5½'' set of black and white penguins is identical. All five have yellow eyes, orange beaks and orange feet. $15-20

Plate 212 Five Navy blue & White Penguins by Kubla Crafts. This 5½'' set of five penguins are all the same. They have navy blue and white bodies, orange beaks and feet and blue eyes. A turquoise line outlines the stomachs. $15-20

Plate 213 Five Navy blue & White Open Flipper Penguins by Kubla Crafts. In this 5½'' set, all five penguins are alike with navy blue and white bodies. The beaks and feet are orange, while the eyes are blue. The open flippers are outlined with both turquoise and orange lines. $15-20

Plate 214 Five Green Frogs by Kubla Crafts. The 5½'' set of five frogs is alike. The frogs have green bodies with white bellies and bright yellow eyes. $15-20

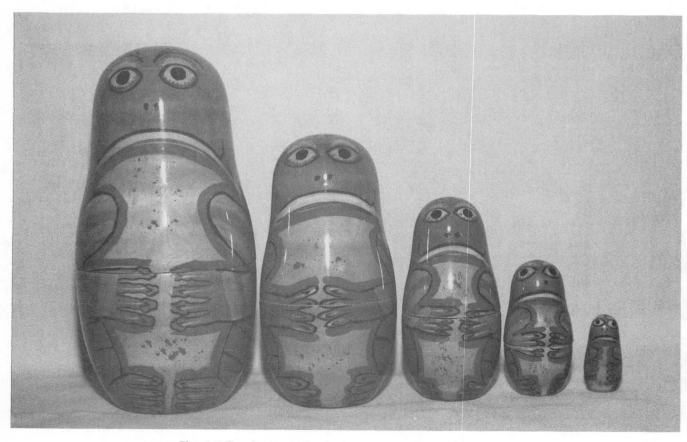

Plate 215 Five Green and Purple Frogs by Kubla Crafts. This 5½'' set of five frogs is tall and narrow. The frogs have pale green skin, beige bellies, yellow and red eyes and purple striped arms. $15-20

Plate 216 Four Soldiers and Three Soldiers by B. Shackman & Co. (Left) This 8'' set of four soldiers is made with a protruding nose. All four soldiers are dressed alike in black helmets, red jackets, white belts and blue trousers. (Right) This 5'' set of three is simple in shape. The orange-haired soldiers have black helmets with uniforms of red, purple, white, blue and pink. $10-20

Plate 217 Three soldiers by Kubla Crafts. This 5½'' set of three soldiers is cylindrical in shape. The soldiers wear black helmets and red uniforms. They have tan hair and red round noses. $10-15

120

Plate 218 Three Patriots by Kubla Crafts. This set depicts the English Duke, Lord Nelson. Nelson is missing his hand in this 5½'' set of three. His white hair is highlighted by his navy blue uniform. $10-15

Plate 219 Three Santas by Kubla Crafts. These 5½'' Santas are dressed in red and white. The trio have white beards with blue lines. Large black belts close their jackets. $10-15

Plate 220 Five Santas by Kubla Crafts. This 5½'' set of five Santas is more narrow than the set of three. Santas have orange faces, white beards with blue lines, and red and white clothing. $15-20

Plate 221 Three Santas. This 5'' set of three Santas is very detailed. The Santas are dressed in red with white trim. They wear green mittens and hold red and white candy canes. They carry dark green sacks over their shoulders. Large green holly sprigs are painted on their backs. ''Happy X'mas'' is painted in yellow on the back of their heads. Rare $20-25

Plate 222 Three Clowns (2 versions) by Kubla Crafts. Both clown sets of three are 5½'' tall. These comical fellows have natural wood faces, yellow caps and costumes of red and green. $10-15

Plate 223 Five Clowns by Kubla Crafts. The circus clown set of five dolls is 5½'' tall. The orange-haired fellows have natural wood faces, green shirts and red trousers. Their large bowties are striped with red and green. $15-20

Plate 224 Three Scarecrows by Kubla Crafts. The scarecrow set of three has a most unusual shape. The dolls open at the neckline. The set is 5½'' tall. The scarecrows have natural wood faces with stringy brown hair. Their old floppy hats are dark brown with yellow patches and yellow rope bands. They wear red shirts, grey shoes and black trousers. The trousers are patched with red and yellow geometric shapes. $15-20

Plate 225 Three Pirates by Kubla Crafts. This set of three is 5½'' with very large natural wood heads. The men have long dark hair in shades of orange, brown and green. Their hair is tied with head scarves of green, yellow and tan. The largest pirate wears a black eye patch, while the middle man smokes a brown pipe. All three hold brown bottles of rum. Their clothing is yellow, orange, green, red and tan. $15-20

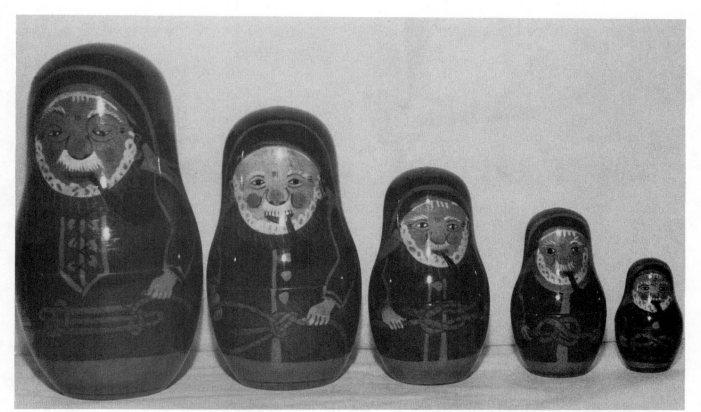

Plate 226 Five Fishermen by Authentic Models Holland. This is the original set of Fishermen. The set is broad and tall – 6'' with five men. The men are all alike in very dark turquoise raingear. The outlines of the clothing, the buttons and the trousers are turquoise. Each fisherman holds a rope tied in a different type of knot. $30-35

Plate 227 Five Fishermen by Kubla Crafts. This set of five fishermen is 5½'' tall. They are painted with dark turquoise raingear. They have long, narrow faces with large noses. Their white beards are scantily painted. All five fishermen hold ropes knotted in different ways. $15-20

126

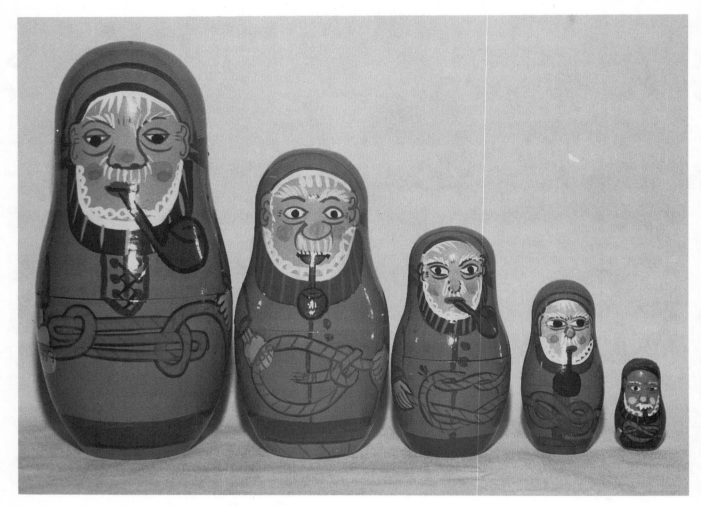

Plate 228 Five Fishermen by Authentic Models Holland. This 5½'' set of five fishermen has all similar men in turquoise raingear. Each man holds a rope which has been tied in different knots. (also pictured as Plate 242 under China section) $19-27

Plate 229 Sheik (2 versions) by Authentic Models Holland. These two 6'' sets of five are quite lovely. (Left) This sheik wears tan, brown and yellow clothing. His wife wears a black dress with a yellow face veil. The son is dressed in yellow, while the daughters are wearing red. (Right) This sheik is garbed in white and black. The four ladies in his harem are dressed in black. Rare $30-35

Plate 230 Eskimo Family by Authentic Models Holland. This is the original set of Eskimos. The set is tall and broad – 6''. The natural wood faces are large and round with dark facial features, red cheeks and lips. All five faces are outlined in white fur. Their clothing is painted in dark shades of browns, blacks and blue with bright highlights. Rare $30-35

Plate 231 Gypsy Family by Authentic Models Holland. This gypsy family of five is 6'' tall. They appear quite rugged with dark skin tones, black hair and eyes. The two largest figures are men dressed in white shirts and dark trousers. The largest man holds a guitar. The largest girl wears a tan blouse and dark skirt. The two small girls wear polka dot dresses – one white and the other red. Rare $30-35

128

Plate 232 Five Sea Captains by Kubla Crafts. This set of five Sea Captains is 5½'' tall. The men have orange faces, grey hair and white beards. They wear royal blue jackets with many orange buttons. Each man wears a white shirt and light blue necktie. All five smoke a black pipe. They wear blue caps with white ovals and black anchors. $15-20

Plate 233 Five Wizard of Oz by Kubla Crafts. Follow the yellow brick road with this five piece set. This 5½'' set includes Dorothy, the scarecrow, the cowardly lion, the tin man and little Toto. Dorothy is a brown-haired beauty with a yellow blouse, blue jumper, white plaid apron and ruby slippers. She holds a woven basket in her hands. The scarecrow has a yellow face and dark brown clothing. The lion is painted in several hues of tan. The tin man is grey and Toto, the dog, is dark brown. $15-20

Plate 234 Six maidens in saris. Traditional maidens make up this 7″ set of six. They have large black eyes and black hair. They wear saris and veils in assorted colors of red, green and orange. $12-15

Plate 235 Six modern Indian maidens. In this modern variation, six maidens complete this 7″ set. The largest doll wears sunglasses. Their black hair is flowing down their backs. All six wear red dresses. Rare $15-20

130

Plate 236 Wobble head family of four. The father in this 9″ set of four has a spring connecting his head to his body. The family members have pink skin, black hair and facial features and red clothing. ''Happy Family'' is painted in white on the front of father. Rare $6-10

Plate 237 Three Maharani by Kubla Crafts. This lovely set of three ladies is 5½″ tall. The natural wood faces of the women are accented with black hair and eyes. They wear green blouses and red veils and saris. The veils and saris are delicately painted in yellow with simple patterns. $15-20

Plate 238 Three "Metrushcha" (Semenov maidens) by Kubla Crafts. This 5½" set of three is an Indian version of a Russian nesting doll. The maidens have natural wood faces and aprons with red flowers painted on the front. They have black hair and facial features. Yellow babushkas with red polka dots cover their heads. Their dresses are red in the typical Russian style. $10-15

Plate 239 Black lacquered maidens. Both sets of seven maidens are 4" tall. These are Indian copies of the black lacquered maidens from the Brest region of the Soviet Union. The maidens have natural wood faces with dark facial features. They wear babushkas of either dark blue or red. The dolls wear capes of red or blue as well. Their dresses are black with red water lilies painted on the front. Rare $15-20

CHINA

Chinese artists invented and created the first nesting dolls early in the last century. The dolls evolved and became fully developed in Russia. It is only fitting that during the height of popularity, the craft returns to its Chinese roots. Yet who could have imagined that dolls now made in China were first designed in Holland!

The company, Authentic Models Holland, has designed an eighteen set collection of nesting dolls in the Netherlands that is now manufactured in China. Originally the company had designed four nesting sets that had been produced in India. Unfortunately, a fire destroyed the factory there. (See chapter on India.) When the company decided to resume operations once again, they chose a new country, China, for production. Some collectors might appropriately regard these nesting doll sets as ''hybrids,'' with their Dutch design, Indian roots and Chinese manufacture. For purposes here, however, the author will consider them to be Chinese.

In approximately 1982, Fishermen and Eskimo sets were first manufactured in India. They continued to produce these sets in China, as well as adding fifteen other sets to the line. The Sheik (two versions – with a family and with a harem), previously produced in India, was dropped from the line. A few Gypsy family sets were made in a very limited series (66) in India, and they were likewise discontinued.

When the manufacturing site was switched from India to China, a few stylistic changes were made. The Indian sets were larger in both height and width. The sets from India have a smoother, high gloss finish. The Indian sets are also better painted. The smallest doll opened in the Indian sets, while the smallest Chinese doll is one solid piece. The Chinese sets are now sold in a cloth, drawstring bag; the Indian sets were not.

The themes of these sets are similar to those of Kubla Crafts of India. A pirate, fisherman and captain and crew set all depict seafaring men. There are two sets of flat headed, cylindrical soldiers that resemble their Indian counterparts in shape and style as well as theme. This collection depicts four sets of bears, panda bears, teddy bears, birthday bears and Goldilocks and the three bears. There are some international families, an eskimo family, a Swiss Tyrol farmer's family, Dutch girls and the English comic, Pierrot. Every set in the collection is quite whimsical and demands close examination. The Jolly Joker is a playing card hand. Santa nests a reindeer as well as elves. Finally inside a set of four cats is a tiny, little mouse!

A spokesman for Authentic Models Holland, Bob Wallace, revealed his company plans to eventually produce a series of 30-40 sets. In May of 1986, Authentic Models Holland (U.S.A.) introduced ten new sets to its series for a total of twenty-six pieces. The company also announced, ''improved 'by hand' production techniques bring new lower prices for the collection.'' The four Indian sets had retailed for $32 per set. The Chinese sets had been selling for $27.50 each. This newest series reduced the price for the sets to $22 retail.

The newest sets in the collection include two eggs. The first set is called a lifetime egg. The set of five eggs begin with a male infant and progresses to a Grandpa. The second set of five animal eggs progresses in size from a small mouse, rabbit, cat, monkey and finally to a dog. Colored egg shells contain each animal as if they are hatching. Nested eggs are a new variation for this company.

The eight new nesting sets all express humor and whimsy, as the other sets have. The Dining Panda is similar to the original panda bear set. He varies only in shape. The dining panda is now squatty like the teddy bears. Authentic Models Holland continues its historical themes with Medieval Knights and Marianne of France. Bear collectors will be happy not only with the new dining panda, but with the Christmas bears as well. The Greatest Show on Earth is a set of circus performers. The largest doll is a tan elephant. Monkey Wisdom is based on the centuries old theme of ''see no evil, hear no evil and speak no evil.'' Two additional chimps complete this simian set. The Wolf and Pigs is based on the nursery tale and a companion set to Goldilocks and the three bears. Last but in some ways, the most exciting, is Your Fortune Telling Dolls. The characters are from a Tarot card deck. This set of six is a companion to the Jolly Joker, the playing card deck set. Many collectors will be thrilled to add these European designed sets to their own collections. The lowered price makes them even more attractive.

In March of 1987, Authentic Models Holland introduced twenty new nesting sets to their already extensive line. The first four sets are the typical five or six piece versions. The new sets include unpainted dolls (6), costume dolls, barrels and a new variation of Dutch girls. In addition to these sets, three egg sets were introduced. Humpty Dumpty is a humorous theme. A world egg and unpainted egg complete this series. The last thirteen sets are new in size. These 3'' sets are less expensive and contain three pieces. Ten of the sets are smaller versions or variations of larger sets in the series. Fishermen, Winning hand, Captain, Santa Claus (with loops for hanging on a Christmas tree), Teddy bears, Cats, Tyrol family, Circus, Revolutionary guard and Farmer girls are variations. Napoleon is a new small set, but related to Marianne de France. Dutch girls are another new small set, but again they are related to the three other Dutch sets. Big Chief with an American Indian, eskimo and seal is a totally new theme in the smaller size. All the new sets are interesting and desirable to collectors.

There is one difficulty in collecting all the sets made by Authentic Models Holland. They have given some companies exclusive rights to sell certain sets. In 1984, the Smithsonian catalog exclusively sold the Fisherman. In 1985, the Pirate was an exclusive set with the Smithsonian. The House of Tyrol, a catalog firm located in Rome, Georgia, sold the Medieval Knights exclusively in 1985, while in 1986 they sold the Tyrol family. The K.L.M. Royal Dutch Airlines are the sole carriers of the Dutch Maidens. In fact, the Dutch Maidens are not even available for public sale. The sets are given to first class passengers of the K.L.M. Royal Dutch Airlines as souvenirs of their flight. They are considered "collector's items" since they are limited in number and distribution. The inventory of the Dutch Maidens remain on the planes themselves. The Cats appeared in two different cat magazines, *Cat Fancy* and *Cat Magazine*. The Authentic Models Holland company eventually gets the exclusives back. However, if you are unaware of who is selling what, you may have difficulty locating the entire line. In fairness to the company, it is possible to receive a price list from Authentic Models Holland. They will sell to collectors direct at full retail price. In this way, you at least know what is being made and if it is available.

Every nesting set in the collection is lathe made by hand from select hardwoods. Each doll is carefully hand painted and varnished. Great care is given to detail, fit and design. The Indian sets, however, were superior in workmanship. These Chinese dolls resemble the Russian sets in shape and almost rival them in workmanship, providing some justification for their rather expensive pricing. The sets are sold in a drawstring cloth pouch, a nice added touch. Some include a certificate of Authenticity as well. The dolls are not recommended as toys for children.

It must be noted here that the Lifetime Eggs and the Dutch Maidens are packaged in green cardboard boxes and plastic. The "boxes" are somewhat misleadingly marked, "Made in Holland." In fact, these dolls are made, along with all of the other sets, in China.

As a group, this highly creative line of nesting doll sets is quite interesting and some sets are truly lovely. They do have room for improvement in the painting and varnishing of the dolls, however. Some are quite textured. The company has plans for expanding the themes chosen. It would be fun to find a set that resembles the first Chinese sets made. We will have to see what the future holds for Authentic Models Holland.

As a footnote, there are small, three inch, blank sets of three nesting dolls made in China. These natural wood sets are sold in craft and hobby shops for the craftsman to paint himself. The individual purchaser is the sole designer. These sets have not been distributed extensively in the United States and are not likely to find their way into many collections.

Plate 240 Packaging by Authentic Models Holland. The white, cloth, drawstring bag has red printing. Pamphlets are printed in red and black.

Plate 241 Green cardboard box by Authentic Models Holland. The dark green box has a light green logo pattern and a plastic slip-over cover.

Plate 242 Fishermen by Authentic Models Holland. This 5½'' set of five fishermen has all similar men in turquoise raingear. Each man holds a rope with a different type of knot. (Also pictured as Plate 228 under India section) $19-27

Plate 243 Eskimo Family by Authentic Models Holland. This 5½'' set of five Eskimos alternates males and females. The males wear black and brown clothing, while the female dress is in shades of blues, black and browns. $19-27

Plate 244 Pirates by Authentic Models Holland. This 5½'' set of five pirates consists of men dressed in dark greens, red, black, white and yellow accents. $19-27

Plate 245 Captain and Crew by Authentic Models Holland. This 5½'' set of five sailors varies greatly. The captain wears a blue jacket, white pants and a white hat with a black bill. The first crewman wears a white hat with black bill, black jacket and white trousers. The second crewman wears a red head scarf, blue and white striped shirt and orange trousers. The cook is dressed all in white and the last mate wears yellow and blue. $19-27

Plate 246 Royal Guard by Authentic Models Holland. This cylindrical set of three soldiers is 5½'' tall. All three wear black helmets. The largest guard wears a jacket of red and yellow. The middle guard wears a jacket of blue with red trim. The small guard wears a green jacket with a white bib. $17-25

Plate 247 Panda Bears by Authentic Models Holland. This set of five bears is 5½'' tall. Each bear is white and black in assorted poses. They are eating green shoots of bamboo. $19-27

Plate 248 Teddy Bears by Authentic Models Holland. This broad set of five bears is 4¼'' tall. Each bear is tan with brown feet. They wear clothing in bright colors of green, white, red and blue. The largest bear holds a red flower, the middle bear holds a green book and the baby bear carries a green and white ball. $19-27

Plate 249 Birthday Bears by Authentic Models Holland. This happy family of five tan bears is 5½'' tall. The father bear wears a white shirt and blue slacks. He holds bright balloons of red, blue, green and yellow. Mama bear, dressed in pink and white, holds a white birthday cake. Brother bear wears a blue suit and sister looks lovely in her bright red dress. Baby bear completes the set in his blue clothes and a yellow bow tie. $19-27

Plate 250 Goldilocks by Authentic Models Holland. This set of five fairy tale dolls is 5½'' tall. Mama, Papa and Baby are brown bears. Papa wears a red jacket, a blue cap and blue pants. Mama's dress is pink and her cap and apron are white. Baby bear wears a blue and red baseball cap and a blue and white dot jacket. Lovely Goldilocks' green dress highlights her long blonde hair. She has also brought her own tan teddy bear. $19-27

Plate 251 Dutch Girls by Authentic Models Holland. This set of five is described as farmer and fishing village Dutch girls by the manufacturer. The 5½'' dolls are dressed in national dresses of Holland. The clothing colors used are bright yellows, reds, blues, whites and black. Each girl wears yellow wooden shoes. Rare. $25-30

139

Plate 252 Pierrot by Authentic Models Holland. The 5½'' set of five depicts the comic Pierrot in his typical garb. The dolls wear white ruffled collars, white shirts and slacks and blue jackets. The make-up is painted in white depicting sorrow and happiness in the same set. Pink flowers are in the arms of the three largest dolls. The dolls have orange hair. The largest Pierrot wears a black felt hat. $19-27

Plate 253 Jolly Joker by Authentic Models Holland. The Jolly Joker is a set of five playing cards. The 5½″ set is made to depict the joker, king, queen, jack and aces. They are all painted white, black, red and yellow. $19-27

Plate 254 Santa Claus by Authentic Models Holland. Jolly old St. Nick and his helpers are 5½″ tall. This set of five starts with Santa dressed in traditional colors of red and white. Next is a tan reindeer. The last three are elves also dressed in red and white. $19-27

Plate 255 Lifetime Egg by Authentic Models Holland. The lifetime set of eggs is 3½″ tall. The five figures reveal different stages of life from old age to infancy. The grandpa and baby are dressed in blue and white stripes. The bald father is dressed in a brown suit. The blonde youth is dressed in green and red. The boy wears blue pants and a yellow shirt. $10-15

Plate 256 Medieval Knight by Authentic Models Holland. These 5½″ knights are a set of five. Each knight is dressed in armor in shades of grey, white and black. Capes on the backs of the knights are painted with medieval symbols. The capes are red and black, green and yellow, blue and red, orange and yellow and yellow and red. $19-27

Plate 257 Christmas Bears by Authentic Models Holland. The bear family of five tan bears has dressed up to depict Christmas figures. The 5½'' set begins with papa bear Santa. Mama bear, dressed in yellow could be a queen bearing gifts. Sister is dressed in white as an angel. Little brother is an elf dressed in green, and baby is a miniature Santa. $19-27

Plate 258 The Greatest Show by Authentic Models Holland. This 5½'' circus set of five begins with either a grey, white or tan elephant. The clown wears red pants, bowtie and cap, and a yellow jacket. The strongman is dressed in pale blue and white. The highwire performer is wearing red with a yellow umbrella. The last piece in the set is a horn player. In some sets the smallest piece is a tan monkey and in others, it is a person dressed in blue and white.
$19-27

Plate 259 Cats and Mouse by Authentic Models Holland. These five cats are made in a 5½'' set. Each one of the four cats has a white tummy. They have fur in stripes of tan, black and orange. The third cat is black and the fourth is a Siamese. The smallest piece is a grey mouse. $19-27

Plate 260 Monkey Wisdom by Authentic Models Holland. This set of five monkeys is 5½'' tall. The largest is a black gorilla daddy holding a black baby. Mama is tan in a green dress holding a tan infant. A black monkey dressed in pink holds another black baby. The last two chimps are tan and white. $19-27

144

Plate 261 Humpty Dumpty by Authentic Models
Holland. Humpty Dumpty is a set of five in this
classic version. Humpty is 3½'' tall, all white
and dressed in brown. All the king's horsemen
and men are garbed in reds, blacks and blues.
The second man sits on a tan horse. $14-25

Plate 262 World Eggs by Authentic Models Holland. The
medieval world is rendered in this 3½'' set of five eggs.
The eggs are black, white, blues and natural wood tones.
$14-25

Plate 263 Small Santa Claus by Authentic Models Holland. This hanging ornament set of three dolls is only 3'' tall. Santa, dressed in red and white, holds a wrapped gift. Santa's helpers are small children dressed in red, white and green. $7-10

Plate 264 Napoleon by Authentic Models Holland. The French revolutionaries don't look so fierce in this 3'' set of three. Napoleon is dressed in his trademark clothing, white vest and trousers, high black boots and black bicorne hat. His long coat is a muted green. The soldier is garbed in an orange band black uniform with a tall black helmet. The small peasant girl is wearing clothing in shades of orange, muted green, pink and white. Other sets sometimes have this small girl dressed in France's national colors of red, white and blue. $7-10

Plate 265 Small Dutch Girls by Authentic Models Holland. In reality this 3'' set is made up of two girls and a boy! The largest girl wears a white, winged Dutch hat, muted green blouse with a large white collar, red and tan apron and striped yellow skirt. The boy's clothing is typical Dutch with a black cap and trousers and striped shirt of white, pink and black. The small blonde girls wears another Dutch costume in shades of white, red, black and magenta. $7-10

Plate 266 Big Chief by Authentic Models Holland. This set of three dolls is only 3'' tall. Big Chief wears a combination of red, white and black. The eskimo is dressed in white and tan. The seal is grey and natural wood tones. $7-10

OTHER COUNTRIES

Russia, Poland, Japan and India are the countries that produce most nesting doll sets. However, nesting dolls are known to originate from other countries as well. In some instances, these sets may be the only design and type manufactured in that country. When an unusual nesting doll set from a unique country is found, it is often interesting to compare it to other sets from the more traditional countries.

Panama in Central America certainly is not known for its nesting doll sets. There is, however, a Panamanian nesting doll set that was primarily made as a souvenir. These sets occasionaly make their way to the United States via tourists who have visited that country. Panamanian nesting dolls very strongly resemble Japanese kokeshi dolls in several respects. The Panama dolls, like their Japanese counterparts, have very large heads. The heads are loosely attached to disproportionately thin bodies, thusly earning their nickname "wobbleheads." Both the Panamanian and Japanese dolls are sold in sets of three male figures or three female figures. Neither Panama nor Japan combine male with female dolls to form a set. In reality, this family of dolls could be considered two separate and distinct sets.

There are some characteristics unique to this Panamanian set. The women wear hair styles that protrude on each side of their heads. Metal and bead earrings dangle from their ears. The men wear flat top "straw" hats. The hues of the paints reflect the natural coloring of the people of Panama. The light tones of their clothing imitate the real culture of this Central American country. This is a lovely and desirable set. Although it imitates the Japanese kokeshi, a true Central American product emerges.

Another Latin country can claim nesting dolls. Argentina in South America engages in a very limited production of nesting doll sets. One Russian family immigrated to Argentina and began a family business of doll-making. While they learned the craft in their native Russia, they adapted it to their new home. This company produces family sets of 4, 5, 6, 7 and 8 dolls, including both male and female members. These mixed combinations are rarely found in Russian sets. The Argentine dolls greatly resemble their Russian counterparts as you might assume. Maidens, Vikings and Easter eggs are also manufactured. The sets are like little jewels, miniature and delicate. It may be assumed that sets such as these, which first appeared in the U.S. early in 1986, will become more readily available in the future.

Germany has a centuries long tradition of fine woodcrafts. The German craftsmen traditionally create nutcrackers, smoking men and small figures. They do not typically lathe turn nesting dolls, nor are they known for their nesting doll sets. Since German woodcrafters are so skilled, it is quite surprising they have not pursued the art form of the nesting doll. Perhaps this is because the Slavic dolls are so foreign to their native Germanic culture.

In the book, *The Story Vine* by Anne Pellowski, she quotes, "Max von Boehn states in *Puppen and Puppenspide* that the nesting doll originated in the studios of the wooden toy makers in and around Munich. Photographs in his book show nesting dolls of peasant women from the first decade of this century that look much more Germanic than the Slavic type we are accustomed to seeing today. Boehn believed the dolls did not 'catch on' in the commercial European market because they made 'a greater appeal to the grown-ups' than to children." Upon examination of the original source, the current author was unable to locate the photos of Germanic nesting dolls. Boehn gives two specific examples of German nesting sets, the Royal family and Snow White and the Seven Dwarfs. The author suggests that perhaps some nesting dolls were produced in Germany, but the Germans were not the first to create the nesting sets. By 1910, the dolls were already produced in Russia. Since the dolls were so Slavic, they did not attract German purchasers.

Even today the author knows of only three German sets, a reflection of their apparent scarcity. Interestingly enough, two of the sets are made of molded plastic, which is a real deviation from the traditional wooden nesting dolls.

The Hermann Eichhorn Company of West Germany has produced two varieties of "The Doll in the Doll" plastic nesting sets. Both sets are sold in Disney World of Orlando, Florida as well as other locations. The first, copyrighted by Walt Disney Productions, is the Donald Duck family. The set is very well made of molded plastic. It consists of six silk screened figures, including Donald Duck, Daisy Duck, Donald's nephews Hughie, Dewey and Louie plus a baby duckling. The duckling is complete with a broken egg shell. This set has great appeal to both Disney fans and children.

A second Eichhorn set is a "Babuschki" maiden family. Like the Donald Duck family, it is well made, heavy plastic, washable, fadeless and silk screened. This doll is a very close copy of the U.S.S.R. classical Semenov Matreshka dolls. The most noticeable difference between the German maidens and the Soviet maidens is the German use of blue. Ironically, this plastic set is more expensive than the original wooden Matreshkas from the Soviet Union.

The third German nesting set is an egg. It is quite simple and lovely but also rather expensive. This wooden egg set is primarily available in the spring as an Easter decoration. It is lathe turned from select hardwoods. Each egg is painted a lovely pastel color and decorated with detailed geometric patterns. The eggs are matte finished and very beautiful.

It is doubtful that many different German nesting sets will be produced. The traditional nutcrackers and smokers remain their first priorities. These three German sets are interesting particularly since they are produced primarily for export.

The Story Vine by Anne Pellowski states that Slavic Czech nesting dolls were made at the turn of this century. This is quite possible, as Czechoslavakia borders on both Poland and the U.S.S.R. However, the author has seen no other references to Czech nesting dolls and has never seen any Czech examples, either old or new. What a wonderful discovery if a collector would find a Czech set!

The Tyrol mountains of Italy house many fine woodcarvers. The house of Anri is probably the oldest and best known Italian woodcarving firm. This company imports many fine woodcarvings to the United States. Anri produced a lathe turned nesting set of cartoon character, Happy Hooligan. Three small, lathe made figures nest inside Hooligan. This set is very rare today. A photograph of this set is shown on page 17 of David Longest's *Character Toys and Collectibles.*

A second nesting doll set has been made in Italy by an unknown manufacturer. This small, primitive set of four maidens is lathe made of hardwoods. The maidens are very simple in form, almost bullet-shaped. The dolls are painted in pale hues of pinks, greens and blues. A bright red color is also used on occasion. The maidens have brown hair with scarves covering their heads. The Italian maidens reflect their U.S.S.R. and Polish influences in both style and dress.

Italian boxes of single nesting dolls are made. On occasion they function as sewing kits, similar to the Russian sets, and as rosary containers. The Italian Noah's Ark, made by Sevi, is quite similar to its Japanese counterpart. It, too, is a crude and simple container. The ark opens to hold flat, jigsaw cut animals as well as Noah and his wife. The Italian ark is larger than the Japanese version, allowing all the pieces to easily fit inside. All Italian nesting dolls and sets are difficult for collectors to locate.

Portugal has produced a plastic nesting doll family of five. This "Chicco" family is quite similar to the Hong Kong set manufactured by Chadwick-Miller. The quality of this set is comparable to the Hong Kong version as well. This set is available in Portugal as a souvenir. This inexpensive family is molded of thin amber colored plastic. The shapes are simple and snap apart. Paper bands are glued on the upper portions of the dolls to define the family members. The "Chicco" family includes a brown haired father with a large mustache and a blonde mother with blue earrings. Inside the mother nests a brown haired big brother, a blonde sister with a large bow and a baby with a blue and white pacifier in her mouth. This set is not readily available in the United States.

Hong Kong is known for its many, inexpensive, plastic exports. The British Crown Colony has manufacted a plastic nesting doll family of seven. It is advertised to give children hours of fun. This "Hideaway Folk Family" was copyrighted in 1983 by Chadwick-Miller, Inc. of Canton, Massachusetts. The sets are sold primarily through catalogs. The colorful shapes are simple, snap-apart pieces. Paper decals provide the details of the family members. The family consists of a five-inch Grandpa, Grandma, Dad and Mom. Inside Mom are neatly tucked her three children – big brother, little sister and a tiny baby. According to a company spokesman, this is the only nesting item Chadwick-Miller produces. Many serious collectors would not include it in their collections.

Korea produces wooden dolls similar to the Japanese kokeshi dolls. The Koreans also manufacture at least two sets of nesting dolls. However, the nesting sets resemble Polish nesting dolls more closely. The Korean artists have created a set of three small clowns and a set of three small penguins. Like Polish dolls, these wooden, lathe made dolls have extended noses or beaks. They are produced and exported as children's toys. However, these two sets are very nicely made. The sets fit well together and are well painted. The Korean sets are of collectible quality.

Taiwan has been called "The World's greatest copier." Two wooden sets made in Taiwan are so close to their Polish originals, that a novice would not be able to tell the difference. Even an expert may need to check the tags that identify the country of origin. These sets are an apple tea set and a soldier bowling set. Once examined, you would find that the tea set is thicker and not as sleek as a Polish set. The soldier set contains ten men instead of the nine in a genuine Polish set. The Taiwan egg, upon examination is plastic! A little knowledge goes a long way if you are collecting only originals.

Some people collect miniatures. Three tiny, Taiwan nesting sets are available. These sets of two and three are inexpensive, simple and even a bit crude. The miniatures include a soldier and a policeman set of three and a clown set of two.

In the 1970's, Kurt S. Adler manufactured two sets of nesting dolls for Santa's World. These Taiwan made dolls were produced for the Christmas market. The Santa Claus and snowman sets of six are simple in form, inexpensive and developed as toys. These two sets, when found, are examples of dolls made in a foreign market exclusively for export. Santa is dressed in the traditional red and white suit of the season. The white ball on the top of his cap is very large. Each Santa is identical except for diminishing size. The snowmen likewise, are very traditional, and are identical except for size.

In 1984, Midwest Importers of Cannon Falls, Inc. introduced a small set of three wooden nesting eggs for the Easter season. The eggs are painted white with pastel stripes around the center. The ends of the eggs are accented with flowers and greenery. This 2½" egg set is still available in the spring. One year later, in 1985, Midwest Importers developed a new line of nesting animal families with a spring theme. The wooden, lathe made figures have accents of felt and ribbon. These sets were designed in American by Cannon Falls, but produced in Taiwan. The animal sets are originals rather than imitations of something else. This line produced high quality families of bunnies, chickens, male cats and female cats. Unfortunately in 1986, the chicks and bunnies were dropped from the line and are no longer available.

Phillip Stahl Imports manufactured two Taiwan nesting sets in 1986. Both sets of four are cylindrical in form and appeal to the Christmas season. Both the Santa and soldier sets contain identical figures within the set. The Santa set includes figures with cone shaped hats decorated with sprigs of holly. They wear the traditional red and white Santa garb. The soldiers are complete cylinders with black helmets and shoes, white trousers and red jackets. Many collectors leave the sets out all year round, despite the Christmas flavor.

Lillian Vernon's 1986 Autumn catalog presented their new, exclusive, wooden soldier. The soldier, made in Taiwan, is a bowling set. The 5½'' soldier, dressed in a blue helmet, red jacket, white trousers and black epaulets holds 10 pins. The tenpins are 1-7/8'' mini-soldiers dressed like the large soldier. The headpin is garbed in opposite colors. Also included are two red wooden balls. The set is recommended for ages five and up.

While the preponderance of nesting dolls originate from Russia, Poland, Japan, China and India, this chapter highlights a number of other counties that make their own distinct contributions to the field. It is reasonable to assume that the number of countries producing nesters will continue to increase as the interest in this form of folk art continues to expand.

Plate 267 Panama, Family of six. The male and female dolls nest separately to form two sets. The sizes range from 5¼'' - ¾''. The males are dressed in white with red, green, blue and yellow accents. The females wear white dresses trimmed in yellow, red and blue. All six members have black hair and brown eyes. "Panama" is painted in black on the front of the two largest dolls. Rare $15-25

Plate 268 Argentina, Family of seven. The family nests as one unit. The largest doll is 5". The family is dressed in muted shades of green, orange and tan. The largest male has white hair, while the other males have brown and blonde hair. The females are blonde. $35-40

Plate 269 Argentina, Families of six. These families nest as one unit. The largest dolls are 3½". The set on the left is dressed in shades of brown and tan. The set on the right is dressed in green, orange and yellow. The largest males have white hair, while the smaller males have brown and blonde hair. The females are blonde. $24-26

Plate 270 Argentina, Egg-shaped blonde maiden sets of four and three. The largest dolls are 2-2½''. The left set is dressed in green, purple and blue. The right set is dressed in pink, turquoise and yellow. $9.50-12.50

Plate 271 Argentina, Blonde maiden set of three. This 2'' set is dressed in green, red and blue. $9.50-12

Plate 272 Germany, Plastic Donald Duck family of six by Hermann Eichhorn Co. The 6½'' set has ducks with white bodies, orange beaks and clothing in shades of blue, pink, red, green and yellow. $15-25

154

Plate 273 Germany, Plastic ''Babuschki'' Maiden family of six by Hermann Eichhorn Co. The 6½'' set has black-haired maidens wearing yellow scarves. The color of their dresses alternates between red and blue. Red flowers decorate the dresses. $15-25

Plate 274 Germany, Pastel nesting egg set of three. The 3'' set is very detailed in pale pink, yellow and purple. $22-25

Plate 275 Italy, Maiden set of four. The brown-haired, 3¼'' dolls are dressed in light blue, pink, green, white and red with yellow buttons. $9-15

Plate 276 Italy, Boxes with sewing kits. (Left) The 2½'' large white and red mushroom opens to hold needles. The mound is green while the rabbit is grey. The elf, flower and bucket are yellow and red. (Right) The 2½'' small, pale yellow box opens to hold sewing items. The tiny figures on top are surrounded by yellow flowers and greenery. The girl wears a blue dress and white apron. The boy wears a green hat, red jacket, white shirt and black trousers. $5-15

Plate 277 Italy, Boxes with rosary case. (Left) The 3″ man with the red hat, white shirt and green jacket opens at his neck. (Middle) The 3¼″ nun is dressed in a dark brown and white habit. She opens at the waist to hold a rosary. (Right) The 2¾″ girl is dressed in a pale yellow, full dress with red dots. She opens at her waist. $5-15

Plate 278 Italy, Noah's Ark by Sevi. The red roof of the 5″ long natural wood ark swings open to reveal flat wooden animals. The animals are painted in pairs of red, green, white, orange and yellow. $7-10

Plate 279 Portugal, Plastic Chicco Family of five. This 5½'' amber toned plastic family has paper labels to provide details. The males have brown hair and the females are blonde. They have blue eyes and clothing accents. The baby sucks a blue pacifier. Rare $10-20

Plate 280 Portugal, Cardboard box for Chicco Family.

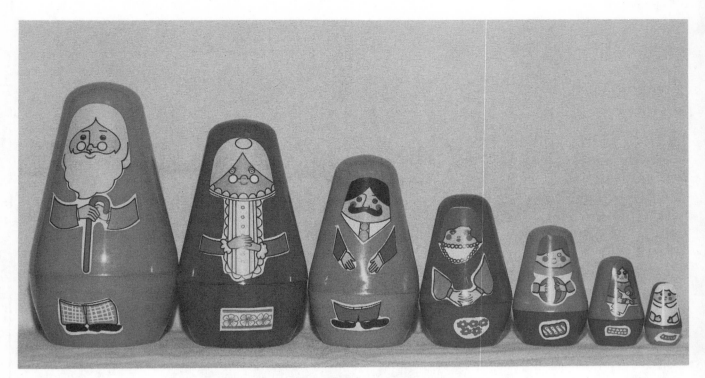

Plate 281 Hong Kong, Plastic Folk Family of seven. This 5½'' multi-colored family provides detail with paper stickers. Grandpa and Grandma, Mom & Dad, brother & sister as well as the baby are blue, yellow, red and green. They have grey, black and brown hair. $3-5

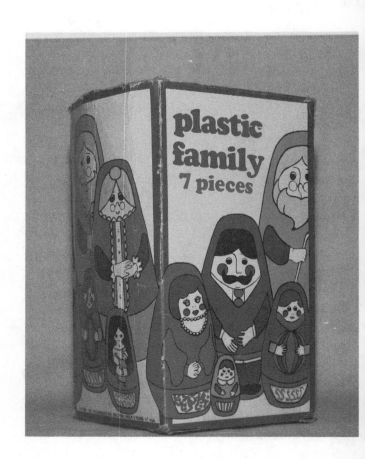

Plate 282 Hong Kong, Cardboard box for Folk Family.

159

Plate 283 Korea, Clowns. This 4¼'' set of three clowns opens at the waist. They have black hair and eyes. The clowns are dressed in red and yellow shirts, blue trousers, black shoes and either green or red hats. $7-10

Plate 284 Korea, Penguins. This 3½'' set of three penguins are identical except for size. They are black & white with orange beaks. $8-10

160

Plate 285 Taiwan, Apple tea set by Lillian Vernon. This set is 3¾'' with a red and yellow apple. Nine pieces fit inside including a red and natural wood table. The natural wood dishes are handpainted with red and green accents. $5-10

Plate 286 Taiwan, Egg & soldier bowling set by Lillian Vernon. The 4½'' plastic egg is hand painted with soldiers dressed in black, red, yellow and white. Two red wooden balls knock down the tenpin soldiers also dressed in the same colors. The kingpin is distinguished by the red tassle on the top of his helmet. $5-10

Plate 287 Taiwan, Miniature clowns & soldiers. These tiny sets are about 1'' tall. The clowns are a set of two, dressed in red, yellow and blue. The soldiers are a set of three, dressed in black, red and blue. $2.50-5

Plate 288 Taiwan, Miniature policemen. This tiny set of three is about 1'' tall. The officers wear black, navy blue and blue. $2.50-5

Plate 289 Taiwan, Santa Claus by Kurt S. Adler. This 5'' set of six are all dressed alike in traditional Santa garb - red and white. Photo - courtesy of The Children's Museum of Indianapolis. $15-20

Plate 290 Taiwan, Cardboard box for Santa Claus. Photo - courtesy of The Children's Museum of Indianpolis.

Plate 291 Taiwan, Striped eggs by Midwest Importers of Cannon Falls. This 2½'' egg set of three is painted in pastel shades of pink, yellow, blue and white. Multi-colored flowers are painted on the ends. $3.50-5

Plate 292 Taiwan, Chickens by Midwest Importers of Cannon Falls. This 5¼'' set of three chickens have felt and ribbon accents. The chickens are yellow with pale pink, purple, blue and green clothing. $10-15

Plate 293 Taiwan, Rabbits by Midwest Importers of Cannon Falls. This 5¼'' set of three white rabbits have felt ears. The father rabbit wears a yellow tie, blue vest and green pants. The mama wears a pink, purple and yellow dress. The child rabbit's clothes have stripes of green, pink and blue. $10-15

Plate 294 Taiwan, Cat families by Midwest Importers of Cannon Falls. These 5¼'' sets of tan, grey and yellow cats nest separately as male and female families. The female cats are dressed in red and yellow skirts and blouses. The male cats wear shirts and trousers of white, blue, yellow and red. $10-15

Plate 295 Taiwan, Santa Claus by Phillip Stahl Imports. The 6¼'' Santa set of four is dressed in red and white. A sprig of holly decorates Santas' hats. These dolls open at the hat. $12.50-15

165

Plate 296 Taiwan, Soldiers by Phillip Stahl Imports. The 6¼'' Soldier
set of four opens at the neck. The soldiers are garbed in red jackets,
black helmets and white trousers. $12.50-15

BIBLIOGRAPHY

Bachmann, Manfred and Hansmann, Claus, *Dolls The Wide World Over*, Crescent Books, a division of Crown Publishers, Inc. (New York) 1973.

Bahar, Ann, "Matreoschka," *Doll Reader*, Dec. 1984/Jan. 1985, pages 138-142, Hobby House Press Inc. (Cumberland, Maryland) 1985.

Bannister, Polly, "The Nesting Instinct," *Yankee Magazine*, pages 189-190, Nov. 1986.

Benet, Sula, *Song, Dance and Customs of Peasant Poland*, Ray Publishers (New York) 1951.

Blinov, Gennadi, *Russian Folk-Style Figurines, A Collector's Notes*, Raduga Publishers (Moscow, U.S.S.R.) 1983.

Boehn, Max von, *Dolls and Puppets*, G.G. Harrap (London) 1932.

Holz, Loretta, *The How-To-Book Of International Dolls*, Crown Publishers, Inc. (New York) 1980.

Longest, David, *Character Toys and Collectibles*, Collector Books (Paducah, Kentucky) 1984.

Munsterberg, Hugo, *The Folk Arts of Japan*, Published with the cooperation of the Japan Society, Inc., New York., Charles E. Tuttle Co. (Rutland, Vermont and Tokyo, Japan) 1958.

Newman, Alex R. and Egerton, *Japanese Art: A Collectors' Guide*, A.S. Bares and Co. (South Brunswick, New York) 1964.

Pellowski, Anne, *The Story Vine*, Collier Books, Macmillion Publishing Co. (New York) 1984.

Poirer Holderbaum, Linda, "The Russian Nested Doll," *Doll Reader*, Aug./Sept. 1985 pages 144-148, Hobby House Press, Inc. (Cumberland, Maryland) 1985.

Pronin, Alexander and Barbara, *Russian Folk Arts*, A.S. Bares and Co., Inc. (Cranbury, New Jersey) 1975.

World Book Encyclopedia, 1983 Edition, "Dolls" Vol. 5-D, pages 234-243, World Book, Inc., A Scott Fetzer Co. (Chicago, London, Sydney, Toronto) 1983.

Pamphlets

Authentic Models Holland, *A Nesting Doll Collection*, (Stamford, Connecticut) 1985.

Authentic Models Holland, *More Nesting Dolls*, (Stamford, Connecticut) 1986.

Authentic Models Holland, *Collection*, (Stamford, Connecticut) 1987

Novoexport, *Matryoshka Dolls* (Moscow, U.S.S.R.).

Shelmar Imports Ltd., *Matrushka*, (Trenton, New Jersey).

Smithsonian Institute, *Nested Dolls*, (Washington, D.C.).

United Nations Gift Center, *Matreshka*, (New York).

APPENDICES

SOURCES

The following is a list of retail stores and catalogs where nesting doll sets can be purchased. This list is far from complete, but is a starting point to locate sets for sale. Some shops have a more substantial supply than others. The late autumn is always a good time to find nesting sets, as they are popular Christmas items.

Many of these retailers are willing to sell via the mail. If you wish to make a purchase, write to the address and request a list of the nesting dolls available at that time. Always include a self-addressed, stamped envelope to insure a response.

The author has written to or purchased dolls from almost every store listed here. There are times, however, when merchants close or change their merchandise. If you don't receive a response, try writing to another retailer. The following shops are listed by state.

Alaska
Russian American Company
407 Lincoln Street
P.O. Box 1030
Sitka, Alaska 99835-1030
(907) 747-3577

Taranoff's Sitkakwan Shop
Katlian Street
Box 1590
Sitka, Alaska 99835

California
The Nature Company
P. O. Box 2310
Berkeley, California 94702
1-800-227-1114

Unicorn Gifts and Toys
3754 The Barnyard
Carmel, California 93923
(408) 625-5086

Canada
Honeymoon Gifts
4943 Clifton Hill
Niagra Falls, Canada L2G 3N5
(416) 357-4330

Florida
Grin and Bear It
P.O. Box 1607
Sanibel, Florida 33957
(813) 472-2552

Mitsukoshi Shop
''Japan'' Epcot Center
Disney World
P.O. Box 40
Lake Buena Vista, Florida 32830

Georgia
House of Tyrol (Catalog Sales)
Gateway Plaza
P.O. Box 909
Cleveland, Georgia 30528

Illinois
Art Institute of Chicago
Michigan Avenue at Adams Street
Chicago, Illinois
(312) 443-3500

Delta Imports
2242 W. Chicago Avenue
Chicago, Illinois 60622
(312) 235-7788

European Imports
Oak Mill Mall
7900 N. Milwaukee
Niles, Illinois 60648
(312) 967-5253

Field Museum of Natural History
Roosevelt Rd. at Lake Shore Drive
Chicago, Illinois
(312) 322-8854

Maison Russe
Russian Curio and Gift Shop
1720 Ogden Ave.
Lisle, Illinois 60532
(312) 963-5160

Museum of Science and Industry
57th Street and Lake Shore Drive
Chicago, Illinois
(312) 684-1414

Russian Bookstore
6347 N. Sacramento
Chicago, Illinois 60659
(312) 338-6644

Indiana
Bittersweet Boutique
Torchlight Village
Box 261
Nashville, Indiana 47448
(812) 988-7877

Cafe Heidelberg
7625 Pendleton Pike
Indianapolis, Indiana
(317) 547-1230

The Children's Museum
P.O. Box 3000
Indianapolis, Indiana 46206

Graham Crackers and other
Collectibles
828 Broad Ripple Avenue
Indianapolis, Indiana 46220
(317) 259-4979

The Indianapolis Museum of Art
1200 W. 38th Street
Indianapolis, Indiana 46208
(317) 924-4951

Kits and Kaboodle
Glendale Galleria
6101 N. Keystone Avenue
Indianapolis, Indiana 46220
(317) 255-3448

The Little House
6515 Carrollton Avenue
Indianapolis, Indiana 46220
(317) 253-8553

Polana Imports International
Old Court House
Crown Point, Indiana 46307
(219) 663-8030

The Toy Chest
58 W. Main Street
P. O. Box 533
Nashville, Indiana 47448
(812) 988-2817

The Toy Shop
8702 Keystone Crossing
Fashion Mall
Indianapolis, Indiana 46240
(317) 846-8778

Kentucky

The Toy Shop
Civic Center Shops
410 West Vine Street
Suite 164
Lexington, Kentucky 40507
(606) 252-TOYS

The Toy Shop
Louisville Galleria
Suite 261
Louisville, Kentucky 40202
(502) 584-TOYS

Louisiana

Crown Colony Clothes,
Gifts and Toys
607 Rue Royale
New Orleans, Louisiana 70130
(504) 525-1177

Michigan

Bronner's Christmas Wonderland
25 Christmas Lane
P.O. Box 176
Frankenmuth, Michigan 48734
(517) 652-8231

The Curiosity Shop
618-B S. Main Street
Frankenmuth, Michigan 48734
(517) 652-8258

Zeesenagel Italian Alpine Village
780 Mill Street
Frankenmuth, Michigan 48734
(517) 652-2591

Minnesota

Polish Import Galleria
P.O. Box 14589
Minneapolis, MN 55414
(612) 331-5121

Ukrainian Gift Shop
2422 Central Avenue North East
Minneapolis, MN 55418

New Hampshire

The Nesting Place
P. O. Box 559
Salem, NH 03079
(603) 893-1251

New York

Babooshka (catalog)
1145 52nd Street
Brooklyn, New York 11219
(718) 633-5309

F.A.O. Schwarz
745 Fifth Avenue at 58th Street
New York, NY 10022
(212) 688-2200

Gingerbread House
9 Christopher Street
New York, NY 10014
(212) 741-9101

Lillian Vernon (Catalog Sales)
510 South Fulton Avenue
Mt. Vernon, NY 10550

U. N. Gift Center
General Assembly Bldg.
1st Ave. and 45th Street
U.N. Headquarters
New York, NY 10017
(212) 754-7700

Ohio

Nine Flags
400 N. High Street
Columbus, Ohio 43215
(614) 464-2149

The Toy Shop
The Westin Gallery
21 East Fifth Street
Suite 108
Cincinnati, Ohio 45202
(513) 721-TOYS

Pennsylvania

Harriet Carter (Catalog Sales)
Dept. 35
North Wales, PA 19455

Texas

Pier 1 Imports (at Christmas time)
2520 W. Freeway
Fort Worth, Texas 76102

Virginia

Kinder Haus Toys
333 Waterside Dr.
Suite 265
Norfolk, Virginia 23510
(804) 625-7942

Washington, D.C.

Smithsonian Institution
P. O. Box 2456
Washington, DC 20013

Wisconsin

Miles Kimball of Oshkosh
(Catalog Sales)
41 West Eighth Avenue
Oshkosh, Wisconsin 54901

Milwaukee Public Museum
800 W. Wells Street
Milwaukee, Wisconsin 53233
(414) 278-2700

Polish Imports Center
4101 W. Greenfield Avenue
Milwaukee, Wisconsin
(414) 384-1442

The Puzzlebox
The Grand Avenue Mall
275 W. Wisconsin Avenue
Milwaukee, Wisconsin 53233
(414) 271-2327

NORWAY

BARENTS SEA

WHITE SEA

FINLAND

U.S.S.R.
(EUROPEAN SECTION)

BALTIC SEA

ESTONIA

OKIROV

VOLGA RIVER

KALININ

LATVIA

SEMENCV
POLKHOV
MAIDAN

YOSCAR-OLA
KAZAN

LITHUANIA

ZAGORSK
MOSCOW

GORKY

WHITE RUSSIA

POLAND

BREST

CZECHOS-
LAVAKIA

HUNGARY

UKRAINE

MOLDAVIA

VOLGA RIVER

RUMANIA

TIRASPOL

SEA OF
AZOV

BULGARIA

CASPIAN SEA

BLACK SEA

TURKEY

IRAN

CHRONOLOGICAL DEVELOPMENT OF NESTING DOLLS

1000 A.D.	Nested Folk Boxes were invented in China.
Early 1800's	Chinese created the first wooden nesting dolls as we know them today. The innermost doll was a grain of rice.
Late 1800's	Russian Artist, Sergei Malyutin sketched the first Russian nested doll. Master carver, V. Zveydochin turned the dolls on a wood lathe, while Malyutin painted the figures.
1900	Zagorsk nesting dolls are exhibited at the Paris World Exhibition. Dealers from all over the world ordered sets, including Americans.
Early 1900's	Semenov craftsmen imitate Malyutin sets and create their own style.
Early 1900's	Vevgenny Bezrukov created a set of 70 dolls, handcarved from a lime tree.
1909	Gogol Centenary souvenir sets made.
1912	A set of dolls was made to commemorate the War of 1812. It ws a set of 8 pieces, depicting Mikhail Kutuzov, a Russian general and hero of the Napoleonic War.
Late 1920's	The inception of the Voznesensk District's (Gorky Region) commercial factory to produce and export lathe made nesting dolls.
1958	The Zagorsk Co-operative Factory won a gold medal for their nesting doll sets at the Brussels Fair.
1967	A set of 50 dolls was sent for exhibit at the Montreal Expo. The dolls became known and popular in the U.S.A., especially the classical Semenov sets.
Early 1970's	The Russian Matreshka sets are sold at the United Nations Gift Shop.
Early 1980's	The Russian Matreshka dolls are very popular in the United States. They are imported and available from many different districts of the Soviet Union.
Mid 1980's	Nesting dolls are imported to the United States from at least thirteen different nations.